China Briefing, 1980

Also of Interest

China's Four Modernizations: The New Technological Revolution, edited by Richard Baum

Chinese Foreign Policy After the Cultural Revolution, 1966-1977, Robert G. Sutter

The Politics of Medicine in China: The Policy Process, 1947-1977, David M. Lampton

Technology, Defense, and External Relations in China, 1975-1978, Harry G. Gelber

China's Quest for Independence: Policy Evaluation in the 1970s, edited by Thomas Fingar and the Stanford Journal of International Studies

The People's Republic of China: A Handbook, edited by Harold C. Hinton

The Chinese Communist Party in Power, 1949-1976, Jacques Guillermaz

China Briefing, 1980

edited by Robert B. Oxnam and Richard C. Bush

Since the death of Mao Zedong (Mao Tse-tung) in September 1976, China's leaders have made breathtaking changes in all areas--politics, economics, foreign policy, culture, and so on. Simultaneously, the island of Taiwan has been undergoing a political evolution in the wake of the termination of formal relations with the United States. This book charts the many changes that have occurred since late 1978. Each chapter, written by a respected China specialist, was originally distributed to U.S. journalists by the China Council of The Asia Society earlier this year. Together, they provide the clearest and most up-to-date analysis of China today.

Robert B. Oxnam, vice president of The Asia Society and program director of its China Council and Washington Center, has lectured and written extensively on Chinese affairs and U.S.-China relations. He is the author of *Ruling from Horseback* and coeditor (with Michel Oksenberg) of *Dragon and Eagle*.

Richard C. Bush, program associate of The Asia Society's China Council and Washington Center, is also editorial supervisor of China Council publications. His dissertation will be published in late 1980 under the title *The Politics of Cotton Textiles in Kuomintang China, 1927-1937*.

China Briefing, 1980

edited by
Robert B. Oxnam
and Richard C. Bush

Published in Cooperation with the
China Council of The Asia Society, Inc.

Westview Press / Boulder, Colorado

Copyright © 1980 by The Asia Society, Inc.

Published in 1980 in the United States of America by
  Westview Press, Inc.
  5500 Central Avenue
  Boulder, Colorado 80301
  Frederick A. Praeger, Publisher

Library of Congress Cataloging in Publication Data
Main entry under title:
China briefing, 1980.
    Includes index.
    1. China--History--1876-   --Addresses, essays, lectures. I. Oxnam,
Robert B. II. Bush, Richard Clarence, 1923-
DS779.2.C44   951.05'8   80-24090
ISBN 0-86531-028-9
ISBN 0-86531-070-X (pbk.)

Composition for this book was provided by the editors.
Printed and bound in the United States of America.

Contents

viii

About the Contributors

Richard C. Bush is a program associate of The Asia Society's China Council and Washington Center. He holds a doctorate in Chinese politics from Columbia University. His dissertation will be published in late 1980 under the title The Politics of Cotton Textiles in Kuomintang China, 1927-1937.

David M. Lampton is associate professor of political science at Ohio State University. He received his doctorate in Chinese politics from Stanford University and is the author of numerous publications, including The Politics of Medicine in China.

Nicholas R. Lardy, associate professor of economics at Yale University, is one of America's leading specialists on the Chinese economy. Educated at the University of Wisconsin and the University of Michigan, he is the author of Economic Growth and Distribution in China. He is currently completing a study on the economics of Chinese agriculture.

Leo Ou-fan Lee is associate professor of East Asian Languages and Cultures at Indiana University. Born in China (Henan province), he was educated at National Taiwan University and at Harvard. He is author of The Romantic Generation of Modern Chinese Writers and articles on modern Chinese literature and history in English and Chinese.

Robert B. Oxnam is a vice president of The Asia Society and director of its China Council and Washington Center. He received his doctorate in Chinese history from Yale University. He is the author of <u>Ruling from Horseback</u> and coeditor (with Michel Oksenberg) of <u>Dragon and Eagle</u>.

Robert A. Scalapino is an authority on Asia and US-Asian relations. Educated at Santa Barbara College and Harvard University, he has taught at the University of California at Berkeley since 1949. His recent publications include <u>Asia and the World Ahead</u> and <u>The Foreign Policy of Modern Japan</u>.

Michael Sullivan, Christensen Professor of Oriental Art at Stanford University, is a leading authority on the art of China. He received his education at Oxford, Cambridge, and Harvard. Sullivan lived in China for five years during the 1940s and visited three times during the 1970s. His books include <u>Chinese Art in the Twentieth Century</u>, <u>The Birth of Landscape Painting in China</u>, and <u>The Three Perfections: Chinese Painting, Poetry and Calligraphy</u>.

Hung-mao Tien is professor of political science at the University of Wisconsin-Waukesha. A native of Taiwan, he studied at Tunghai University and the University of Wisconsin. He is the author of many publications in Chinese and English, including <u>Government and Politics in Kuomintang China</u>, and editor-columnist for the Taiwan newspaper <u>Taiwan Shihpao</u>.

Foreword

The China Council of The Asia Society was
formed in the summer of 1975. The idea was that
mixing scholars, journalists, businessmen and other
laymen interested in China would enrich the public
dialogue on the development of Sino-American relations. Since its formation the Council, working
increasingly through a network of affiliated regional councils with a similar membership mix, has
tried to meet the steadily rising demand for information about China.

From the beginning one of the Council's main
chores has been to brief US journalists who were
suddenly required to report on a country, and a
civilization, about which they knew little or
nothing. The Council's scholars have protected
scores of us in the news business from embarrass-
ment -- and they have protected our readers and
listeners from the errors we would have otherwise
committed in covering the China story.

Those of us who have used these essays, and
others produced earlier, are indebted to the
scholars who wrote them and to the Council staff
which got them to us, often on very short notice.
We owe a special debt to three men -- John Fair-
bank, Jerome Cohen, and Doak Barnett -- who led the
China Council through its first years. Their support for those who must daily compose that "first
rough draft of history" has lightened our load --
and enlightened our work.

Charles W. Bailey

Minneapolis

Acknowledgements

It is with great pleasure that we acknowledge a number of individuals who assisted us in preparing China Briefing, 1980 and have supported the broader educational effort of which it is a part:

--the authors, whose chapters were initially prepared as China Council briefing essays for American journalists.

--members of the China Council and others who reviewed chapters in draft form.

--past and present colleagues at The Asia Society's Washington Center and China Council: Terrill E. Lautz, who edited the chapters on art and literature; Jonathan Daen, Daisy Kwoh, Elizabeth Nichols, Susan Rhodes, Judith Sloan, and Lisa Swanberg, all of whom helped in a variety of ways.

--Pat Malloy of The Asia Society and Shen Fu of the Freer Gallery of Art, who assisted us in securing visual material.

--Harry Harding, Kenneth Lieberthal, and David M. Lampton, all of whom contributed to the biographical appendix.

--Nicholas Lardy, who prepared the appendix of economic statistics.

--Martha Bush, who helped with proofreading.

--those who provide crucial guidance to The Asia Society's China Council: Council Co-chairmen Charles W. Bailey, Irv Drasnin, and Ezra F. Vogel; and The Asia Society's president, Phillips Talbot, and executive vice president, Lionel Landry.

--Frederick A. Praeger (our publisher), Lynne Rienner (our editor), and their able associates at Westview Press.

Without their help and support, we would have

had to take responsibility for many more errors than those that inevitably remain.

Robert B. Oxnam
Richard C. Bush

Washington, D.C.

A Note on Romanization

How to render Chinese words into written English has been the subject of a long debate. Politics and linguistic theory are both involved.

For many years, the Wade-Giles system, devised by two nineteenth-century British diplomats, was the standard for all but names of prominent places. These were rendered in the Postal Atlas system (for example, Peking in the Postal Atlas system is Peiching in Wade-Giles). Both systems had their share of anomalies, and a number of alternatives were proposed over the years. One of these, called pinyin (literally "phonetic spelling"), was adopted by the People's Republic of China for limited internal use in the late 1950s. But in its publications distributed in the English-speaking world, the PRC, like the Nationalist regime on Taiwan, retained the Wade-Giles and Postal Atlas systems.

That situation ended on January 1, 1979, when the PRC switched to pinyin for its foreign publications. True to its name, pinyin is more phonetic than its predecessors, but does introduce some new anomalies. Meanwhile on Taiwan, the Nationalists have continued with Wade-Giles, for obvious reasons.

We prefer to remain neutral in the romanization debate, and in this volume will follow the Chinese maxim, "observe the customs of the district in which you sojourn" (i.e., "When in Rome . . ."). We adopt the following convention:

--pinyin is used when referring to people associated with the Communist movement and to people and places under PRC jurisdiction.
--Wade-Giles is used when rendering names of individuals associated with the Nationalist regime

and names and places now under Nationalist control
(with the exception of the familiar Cantonese ren-
derings for Sun Yat-sen and Chiang Kai-shek).
    --where a living individual prefers an anoma-
lous spelling, that preference is observed (as in
Chen Jo-hsi and Lee Huan).
    --any remaining names are rendered in <u>pinyin</u>.

    By and large, therefore, chapters dealing with
events in the PRC employ <u>pinyin</u>, and the chapter on
Taiwan uses Wade-Giles. Appendix C (beginning on
page 119) provides a detailed conversion table.

Source: US Department of State, "Background Notes:
China," March 1980. The dotted line de-
notes the July 1, 1979 expansion of Inner
Mongolia (Nei Monggol), whereby the auton-
omous region received the western portions
of Heilongjiang and Jilin provinces, and
the northern portions of Liaoning and Gan-
su provinces and of the Ningxia Hui Auton-
omous Region. This change restored the
borders existing before July 1969.

1
Introduction

Robert B. Oxnam

China Briefing, 1980 is designed to provide an up-to-date overview of contemporary China for the interested layperson. The book is a spin-off of the media activities of The Asia Society's China Council. For several years the Council has commissioned talented China watchers to prepare concise background papers for print and broadcast journalists. It is clear -- from the hundreds of requests for reprints -- that the demand for this type of information extends far beyond the American media, to corporate executives, college and university students, high school students and teachers, members of public and world affairs organizations, and the thousands of tourists who visit China each year (some 40,000 in 1979). The Council is pleased that Westview Press is publishing this volume (the first in an annual series), which includes the background papers written or revised in the spring of 1980.

China was in the headlines throughout 1979 and early 1980. The period began with the normalization of Sino-American relations on January 1, followed closely by Vice Premier Deng Xiaoping's much-publicized trip to the United States. It was a year in which the post-Mao Chinese leadership consolidated itself and sharpened its attack on many of Mao's former colleagues and policies. It was a year when the Chinese took a sober look at their modernization policies and started emphasizing slower growth, careful planning, and more individual incentives. It was a year of continued openness to the outside world with diplomatic missions to Europe and Asia, students in large numbers to advanced industrial countries including the United States (some 1,500 in the US by early 1980), and a

1

30 percent increase in foreign trade. It was also
a year of great dangers on China's frontiers, beginning with the Sino-Vietnamese border war in February and concluding with great concern over the
Soviet invasion into Afghanistan in December. And
it was a year in which the island of Taiwan had to
rebound from the shock of US derecognition.

China Briefing tries to put this whirlwind of
events into perspective by relying on the insights
of several outstanding specialists on Chinese affairs. The book covers a broad spectrum of today's
China -- including leadership, politics, economics
and trade, art, literature, foreign policy, and developments in Taiwan. Each specialist mixes a suc-
cinct review of current affairs with broader analysis of implications for China and China's roles in
the world.

We begin with a short interpretative biography
of the most powerful figure in China today, Communist Party Vice Chairman Deng Xiaoping. This essay, written by Richard C. Bush of The Asia Society, describes the political ups and downs of this
hard-headed advocate of rapid modernization who was
twice purged in the Maoist era. Bush portrays the
76-year-old Deng as a leader with varied experience
whose revolutionary roots can be traced back to the
early 1920s. In the late 1970s Deng masterminded
the building of a post-Mao leadership group and has
even begun to prepare for his own retirement from
politics. As Bush notes, the next few years will
be a tough test for Deng as he seeks to have his
followers and his strategies outlive his own rule.

With Deng introduced, the book moves on to the
broader political context in which he operates, as
described by David M. Lampton of Ohio State University. It would be hard to exaggerate the transformation of recent years -- the purge of most advocates and policies of Mao's Cultural Revolution,
the revival of once-prominent figures attacked in
the late 1960s, and the emergence of somewhat
younger leaders (by Chinese standards) from national and provincial bureaucracies. Lampton analyzes
this coalition's approach to modernization, based
on the principle of "equity," which rewards superi-
or performance even at the expense of social equality. He traces this policy through new patterns of
wages, investment, health care, and birth control.
We also watch Beijing's vacillating policies on intellectual freedom symbolized by the widely heralded "democracy wall" which flourished in early
1979 only to be closed down later in the year. All

of this underscores the truly monumental tasks fac-
ing Chinese politicians, and it prompts Lampton to
remind us that if the leadership fails to bring
greater prosperity to the Chinese people, "it may
find it difficult to keep Mao buried."

Politics and economics have become closely in-
tertwined in the post-Mao era. The year 1979 certainly underscored the fact as the new leadership
grappled with some of the knottier questions con-
fronting modernization and initiated a "readjustment policy" on the economic front. The new policy, analyzed by Nicholas R. Lardy of Yale University, stresses consumption over investment by laying
emphasis on wage increases, consumer goods, housing, and food production. Some may be surprised to
learn that China, once heralded as a model for developing countries, now suffers from serious unemployment and inflation. Business executives may be
relieved to learn that China is still giving strong
attention to foreign trade and investment, but with
more realistic projections and more attention to
the problems of implementation. Lardy makes the
important point that future Chinese political battles will probably center on economics. Differing
viewpoints on China's modernization will yield differing answers to China's economic needs.

The remarkable changes in Chinese politics and
economics have been paralleled by a dramatic opening in the worlds of art and literature, as discussed by Michael Sullivan of Stanford University
and Leo Ou-fan Lee of Indiana University. Both
describe the post-Cultural Revolution "thaw" in
Chinese cultural circles and particularly the renewed work of the senior generation of writers and
artists. Painters and sculptors are once again ex-
perimenting with more individualistic approaches
drawn from Chinese tradition, from the pre-Cultural
Revolution era, and from outside China. Poets,
novelists, short story writers, and playwrights are
producing an array of new works which often play on
the themes and the spirit of the early twentieth
century to counteract the cultural sterility of the
1960s and 1970s.

Thus China seems to be undergoing a "cultural
revolution" quite different from that of the Maoist
period. But will it really last? Will it pene-
trate deeply into the younger generations? Will it
lead to enduring connections with the outside
world? These questions, raised by both Sullivan
and Lee, haunt the creative communities in China.
From the outside, we see new trends which give rise

to Western optimism about China -- a new serious-
ness about education, expansion of universities,
the revival and growth of the Chinese academies
dealing with science and social science, the resur-
gence of religion in several cities. We can even
see the more popular signs of openness -- a craze
for studying English language, Western style clothing, foreign movies, disco music, even disco
skating. But Westerners must be careful, as Sullivan and Lee warn us, to avoid assuming that such
trends will continue without reversals in the years
ahead. To some extent these cultural issues have
analogues in the economic sphere, where the Chinese
seek to maintain their sense of identity while making selected use of Western technology.

A similar note is sounded by Robert A. Scalapino of the University of California when he turns
attention to China's world roles and observes that
"domestic and foreign policies are intimately
linked, as China begins a massive modernization effort." In the 1970s, China acquired a new sense of
confidence in foreign affairs as it was admitted to
the United Nations and recognized by Japan, the
United States, and a host of other nations. In the
post-Mao era, the foreign policy has been motivated
primarily by a quest for security against the Soviet Union and a quest for modern technology from the
advanced industrial world. Ideology has played a
diminished role as China seeks to build a new coalition of support in Western Europe, Japan, Southeast Asia, and the United States. But this past
year has also underscored the risks in China's new
foreign policies, particularly the border conflict
with Vietnam and the renewed harshness in Sino-
Soviet relations.

We next focus in on the island of Taiwan. In
1979, as part of the normalization agreement with
Beijing, the United States ended its recognition of
the regime on Taiwan and announced the termination
of the 1954 mutual defense treaty. Today Taiwan
seems to have survived the shock rather well -- the
domestic economy and foreign trade have grown considerably. Extensive post-normalization ties with
the United States persist, and there is no apparent
outside threat in the near future. But it appears
that the changes in Taiwan's international situation may have had significant consequences for the
island's political future. Hung-mao Tien of the
University of Wisconsin-Waukesha points out several
tensions -- the debate within the ruling Nationalist Party over the future political role of the is-

land's Taiwanese majority, the struggle over succession to Chiang Ching-kuo, and the conflict between the Nationalists and politically active Taiwanese. Tien analyzes each of these trends in light of the Kaohsiung Incident which occurred in December 1979 and the trials that followed.

So that is the scope of China Briefing in its inaugural year. As we can see, the book is designed to offer ways of thinking about China. Through the eyes of various specialists, we sense not only the goals, but also the tensions, underlying contemporary Chinese affairs. By juxtaposing goals and tensions, the nonspecialist can engage in some China watching as well. For instance:

--political unity vs. political resistance: Much of the post-Mao political process has been aimed at restoring unity after the topsy-turvy years of the Cultural Revolution. At the top of Chinese politics, the recovery process has yielded a new modernizing group and new emphasis on Party unity and loyalty. Will the middle and lower reaches of the bureaucracy really adhere to the new economic guidelines or will they bide their time more cautiously? What about the ghost of Mao -- will the process of de-Maoification continue in the years ahead, or will disgruntled elements try to revive a more radical vision of revolution?

--rapid modernization and its obstacles: While the present government steadfastly adheres to its overarching goal of "comprehensive modernization by the year 2000," the policy of "readjustment" is more realistic in admitting obstacles that must be overcome. On one level, we see built-in impediments -- uncertain oil reserves, manpower deficiencies, transportation and energy bottlenecks. On this same level exists the huge built-in problem of China's population -- now officially over one billion people -- a problem that has brought some interesting solutions in recent years, but one that will continue to slow down modernization in the years ahead. On another level, we see the political difficulties as various groups -- industrial planners, agricultural interests, consumer pressures, and military modernizers -- begin to fight over limited funds . In examining these tensions, one is reminded that China is not monolithic, but rather has a great variety of interests operating within the context of a centralized political system.

--the haves and the have-nots: Mao frequently

linked revolution and egalitarianism, most particularly in the policies and rhetoric of the Cultural Revolution. But now, as several specialists observe, rapid economic development has overshadowed egalitarianism as the central goal. Modernization will inevitably promote the interests of certain parts of the Chinese society -- factory workers and managers in large enterprises, intellectuals and teachers, government and Party bureaucrats, students at higher levels, and in general, the 20 percent of the population living in the cities. But it will also create "losers" -- rural officials and teachers, rural students, and in general, much of the 80 percent of the population living in the countryside. Among the biggest losers are the tens of millions of former Red Guards (now in their twenties and thirties) who have lots of revolutionary memories but little power and prestige. Deng and his successors will have to be very adept at dealing with these have-nots lest they become sources of opposition.

--dragons and polar bears: The Chinese face some critical choices in foreign policy and military policies. Will they modernize their military forces rapidly and try to narrow the gap with the superpowers? Or will they place higher priority on industrial and agricultural modernization, and thus shore up their defenses with "quick fixes" from Europe and the United States? Behind this choice is another: how to deal with the Soviet "polar bear." Will they continue to use diplomatic and economic means to build an anti-Soviet coalition? Will they use direct military action, such as in Vietnam, or will they perhaps see that kind of intervention as counterproductive? Might they seek a modest rapprochement with the Soviets, designed to cool border tensions and thus to concentrate on domestic modernization?

--Chineseness vs. Westernization: Many groups in China now seek contact with Japan and the West -- for technology, better education, cultural variety, consumer goods, and more openness in political life. But there are other groups, rather quiet for the moment, which still fear that the capitalist world will contaminate their culture and thus undermine their mix of socialism and nationalism. In the past century, doors tentatively opened have been slammed shut. Will they again?

Given these many competing goals and tensions, the China story is certain to be as fascinating over the years ahead as it has been in the past.

Although China Briefing will not permit readers to
predict the future, it tries to offer greater understanding of the recent past, the contemporary
scene, and possible options for the 1980s.   If
readers recognize more clearly how China's goals
and tensions -- political, economic, social, cultural, and foreign -- are interrelated, then the
book will have served its purpose.

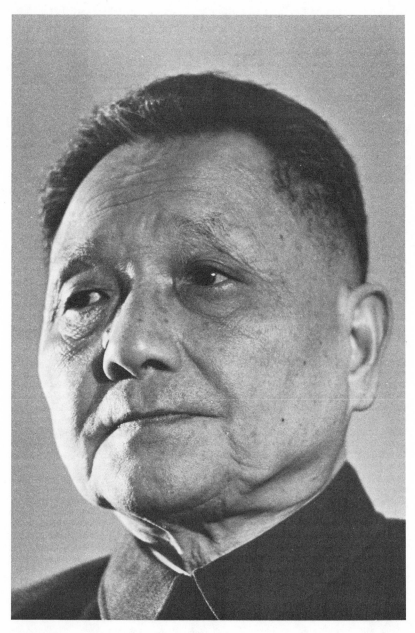

Deng Xiaoping (Sygma)

2
Deng Xiaoping:
China's Old Man in a Hurry

Richard C. Bush

INTRODUCTION

Early in 1980, an elderly man with a weathered yet boyish face addressed 10,000 members of China's ruling elite in Beijing's Great Hall of the People. From his short stature (about five feet), his wooden oratory, and the absence of any intellectual acrobatics, one would not suspect him of being an imposing political figure. Indeed, he began his speech with characteristic Chinese humility, suggesting that his proteges had pushed him to the podium and admitting that "there are . . . certain problems which I cannot speak about very well."[1]

But his listeners knew otherwise. They knew that the title of the speech -- "On the Current Situation and Tasks" -- is reserved in the Communist universe for only the brightest stars. They knew that the speech conveyed political principles that differed sharply from those of the late Party Chairman Mao Zedong.

Futhermore, they knew that the speaker, Deng Xiaoping, had achieved his preeminent position against the worst odds: two purges in ten years at the hands of Mao and his radical adherents; resistance by younger leaders who did not share Deng's view that Mao's Cultural Revolution had been a disaster; and the obstacles of ideological dogmatism and bureaucratic routinization. They also knew that Deng, for all his remarkable persistence, was racing against the clock of his own mortality and of China's immense economic problems. Only time would tell if Deng's vigorous attempt in his final years to put indelibly his own stamp on China's modernization would succeed or fail.

The Dengist approach, enunciated in early

1980, had three related elements. First was the
fundamental task of economic development -- the
four modernizations -- for solving China's problems. Development, not sloganeering or vast social
movements, was the "new revolution" the country
should pursue for the foreseeable future. "If a
revolution," Deng said, "is divorced from the development and modernization of production -- on
which after all the prosperity of any people
depends -- then the aim and goals of this revolution are mere empty words."[2] But Deng warned that
such goals cannot be achieved overnight:

> With the foundation it has, its huge popula-
> tion and its small area of arable land, China
> cannot achieve a large and rapid increase in
> labor productivity, financial [investment]
> income, and imports and exports. Also, the
> people's income cannot grow rapidly. . . .
> [W]e can only catch up with the developed
> countries by long-term efforts.[3]

Moreover, achieving other goals -- international
influence and the unification of Taiwan -- were
contingent on substantial economic growth.
    Second, Deng asserted that China would win the
economic race only by broadening its contacts --
especially economic and technological -- with the
outside world. At the same time, he was confident
that the country would not drift from its cultural
and psychological moorings. He admitted that "we
must rely primarily on our own resources and our
own efforts." He cautioned against "worship of
capitalist foreign countries," being "corrupted and
seduced by capitalism," and losing "the national
pride and self-confidence of socialist China."[4]
Within these limits, foreign contacts were essential:

> In no country has the process of modernization
> occurred in isolation. It has always depended
> on cross-fertilization among different peo-
> ples. . . .[T]he managerial skills of the
> capitalist countries -- particularly various
> methods of developing science and technology
> -- are part of man's common heritage. There
> is no reason why these skills cannot be put to
> good use in a socialist China.[5]

    Third, Deng was firm in his belief that China
could solve its problems through the correct kind

of political guidance. He retained a Marxist faith
in a Communist Party that is a "united force with a
high degree of awareness and discipline" that can
"gather together the strength of the whole people
. . . to achieve tremendous accomplishments."[6]
    But, Deng believed, effective Party rule was
predicated on certain conditions. On the one hand,
there needed to be continuous maintenance of the
organizational machine, by training Party members
to be selfless models for the whole society; maintaining internal discipline; and by selecting Party
cadres who combine both authority and expertise as
leaders of various social institutions. On the
other hand, the Party had to be protected from
harmful external disruption -- like the Great Leap
Forward and the Cultural Revolution -- which Mao
Zedong fostered as an alternative to bureaucratic
administration. Deng also opposed political dissidents attacking the existing system out of a "blind
faith in democracy." He hoped to keep political
criticism within organizational channels, and to
foster more "liveliness and vigor" among the people. However, he asserted, "liveliness and vigor
can only be attained under the premise that stability and unity are not hindered. . . . [T]urmoil can
lead only to retrogression, not progress, and that
progress can only be achieved if there is order."[7]
    The elements of Deng's approach to moderniza-
tion -- economic growth, learning from foreign
countries, and ruling by organization -- all reinforce his pragmatic style. It is an approach and
style quite in conflict with that of Mao -- at
least the elderly Mao of the Cultural Revolution --
and thus Deng suffered considerably in the 1960s
and 1970s. He was purged in the fall of 1966, returned to the leadership in 1973, but was purged
again in April 1976 because he and Mao continued to
disagree on fundamental principles. Deng was reinstated in July 1977, ten months after Mao's
death. Since then he has struggled at length to
contest the Maoist legacy: purging some of Mao's
associates from the Politburo; rehabilitating nearly everyone (living and dead) who ran afoul of Mao,
including Liu Shaoqi, the Cultural Revolution's
most famous victim; instituting policies that ac-
cord with his own modernization approach; reviving
the pre-Cultural Revolution institutional structure; and challenging what he sees as the dogmatism
of Maoist ideology.
    When he returned to power in July 1977, he
confided that he could have done otherwise: "There

are two ways I can go in the future -- working or
becoming an official" [with only ceremonial func-
tions]. If Deng's adversaries were suggesting that
he take the latter course, he refused to accept
their advice. As he said, somewhat disingenuously,
"Naturally, it is easier to be an official than it
is to work, but I am a member of the party and I
must do what the organization assigns me. The party would never ask me to be an official and to do
nothing, and I am not that type of person."[8] That
he did return to "work" is a mark of his ambition,
persistence in the face of obstacles, and deep commitment to his principles -- qualities that have
characterized his entire remarkable career.

DENG THE REVOLUTIONARY (1920-1949)

Deng Xiaoping was not his original name. He
was born Gan Zegao, into a landlord family in the
western province of Sichuan on August 22, 1904. It
was twenty years later, on entering the Chinese
Communist Party, that he took as his revolutionary
name Deng Xiaoping. His birthplace was a small
village near the riverine county town of Guangan,
located about 60 miles from Chongqing, a major commercial center on the Yangzi River. Deng's mother,
one of his father's four wives, also bore a daugh-
ter and two other sons (both of whom were later
Communist officials).

That the young Deng Xiaoping should be both a
Communist and a landlord's son is not particularly
surprising. A great majority of the post-1949 Chinese Communist leadership were sons of landed and
scholarly elites who ended up serving China by "be-
traying" their class. "We felt," Deng later related, "that China was weak and . . . we wanted to
make her strong. We thought the way to do it was
through industrialization. So we went to the West
to learn." Deng went to France, and was soon drawn
into the Communist movement along with Zhou Enlai
and others. (Deng's memory of that formative experience may be a partial stimulus for the current
program whereby thousands of Chinese students and
scholars are abroad studying, primarily science and
technology.)

Deng must have been a precocious student. Before turning sixteen, he had finished high school,
completed a one-year foreign study training program, and arrived in France as an overseas student.
He was later described as "a living encyclopedia,"
"highly articulate," with a mind "as keen as mus-

tard."[9] Once in France, he chose to work in a factory in Lyons and engage in political activities among expatriate Chinese workers. He joined the China Socialist Youth League (a precursor of the Communist Youth League) in 1922, and was involved in propaganda work, earning the nickname "doctor of mimeographing." In 1924 at the age of twenty, he became a member of the Chinese Communist Party.

By the mid-1920s, China was immersed in revolutionary struggle. The Nationalist Party of Sun Yat-sen and Chiang Kai-shek, assisted by the Soviet Union, was building for a fight to the finish with warlords who controlled most of the country. The Communist Party, allied with the Nationalists, called home it members studying abroad to enhance its growing strength.

Deng Xiaoping was part of that flow and, like many others, stopped in Moscow for several months of intensive training. Back in China, he was assigned to do propaganda work in the army of northern warlord Feng Yuxiang. Feng, who had indoctrinated his troops with Christianity using a fire hose to perform mass baptisms, was trying to shore up his tenuous military position by allying with the Nationalists. In return for Soviet assistance, he had to accept political instructors like Deng. But like Chiang Kai-shek, Feng turned against the Communists in mid-1927, and Deng was forced to flee. He went to Shanghai and worked for two years in the underground.

Nationalist control of the cities after 1927 made it more and more difficult for the Communist Party to implement the conventional Bolshevik strategy of mobilizing worker uprisings. Emphasis gradually shifted to building guerrilla bases in rural areas. In mid-1929, the Communist headquarters in Shanghai dispatched 25-year-old Deng Xiaoping to the southwestern province of Guangxi to take charge of the growing guerrilla movement there. He led a series of unsuccessful revolts, and he and his forces had to fight their way overland to join Mao Zedong's forces in Jiangxi province.

Some observers believe that Deng's arrival in Jiangxi in mid-1931 marked a critical point in his career, for he became "one of a small group of men . . . who might legitimately be deemed as Mao's personal clique."[10] Along with Mao, Deng suffered in an internecine struggle in 1933. As he recalled in 1977, "When I followed Chairman Mao [at that time] . . . I was knocked down. I came up again when Chairman Mao won the struggle."[11] Deng accompanied Mao on the Long March of 1934-1935, probably serving as director of the principal military unit's political department.

His relationship with Mao may well account for the important role Deng played once war with Japan began in 1937. He became political commissar of the 129th Division, one of the three divisions of the Communist Eighth Route Army that engaged the Japanese in North China. Aside from indoctrination, he was also responsible for organization, logistics, and recruitment. His assignment may have had an ulterior motive. Many of the officers staffing the 129th Division had not been especially close to Mao, and the Chairman may have wanted Deng to insure their loyalty. In any case, the young commissar soon won the trust and respect of his new comrades, especially that of division commander Liu Bocheng. Like Deng, Liu was a native of Sichuan, and "reputedly held him [Deng] in such esteem that he would embark on no military operation without his first permitting Teng [sic] to assess both its political and military implications."[12]

The forces under the two Sichuanese grew into a large military machine, and provided Deng with the power base to later propel himself, with Mao's endorsement, into the national political limelight. Once the war with Japan ended and the civil war with Chiang's Nationalists had begun, the Liu-Deng units -- renamed the Second Field Army -- moved out of their mountainous base area. They fought a number of important battles, including the critical Huai-Hai engagement in East China in late 1948, which turned out to be the beginning of the Nationalists' end. In 1949-1950, the Second Field Army occupied Southwest China, and the two men took charge of their home province and three others. There were about 300,000 troops under their command.

DENG THE ADMINISTRATOR (1950-1966)

Establishing military control in 1949 was only the first step for the Communist victors. There were new problems to address: determining the balance of power between central and regional governments, building new political institutions, rehabilitating and collectivizing the economy, formulating a strategy of economic development, remolding social values, and fashioning a succession to Mao Zedong. Leadership debate over these issues grew more intense as time went on, and Deng Xiaoping was a central figure in most of th con- flicts. His power grew quickly, but he made the critical mistake of alienating Mao in the early 1960s, and thus became a target of vitriolic crit- icism and purge when the Cultural Revolution began in 1966.

Deng took his first major step up the post-1949 political ladder in 1952. A conflict had erupted over the proper division of power between Beijing and regional Party leaders, especially re- garding implementation of the First Five Year Eco- nomic Plan. When the more advanced northeast and east regions opposed a reduction in their autonomy, Mao mobilized the support of leaders in less wealthy areas, including Deng Xiaoping and Liu Bo- cheng in the southwest. Along with many other re- gional leaders, Deng moved to Beijing and was named a vice premier in Zhou Enlai's cabinet in August 1952. A year later, he became minister of finance.

Deng's next advance up the hierarchy came quickly. Mao moved him out of the field of econom- ics and into that of Party organization. In May 1954, he became secretary general of the Central Committee, supervising the Party's assumption of a new role -- directing the development of a social- ist state and economy. One year later, Deng en- tered the ruling Politburo. His power further increased at the 1956 Eighth Party Congress, where he presented a major report on revisions to the Party Constitution, the first in eleven years. He was advanced to the Politburo's six-man standing (i.e. executive) committee, and was given the new and more powerful post of Party general secretary, in charge of day-to-day policy implementation. By age 52 -- relatively young for a Chinese Communist leader -- Deng was one of the most powerful indi- viduals in China.

Mao Zedong's continuing confidence in Deng's loyalty and ability may have been an important fac- tor in the latter's rise. Once in the mid-1950s, during a meeting of Chinese and Soviet leaders, Mao is reported to have pointed Deng out to Nikita Khrushchev and said, "See that little man there? He is highly intelligent and has a great future ahead of him." For his part, Deng seems to have been unusually responsive to Mao's concerns. He was one of the few Party administrators who sup- ported Mao's call to "let a hundred flowers bloom" -- for criticism of the Communist Party. Even in the early 1960s, Deng apparently supported the

Chairman in his growing conflict with the Soviet Union.

But Mao and Deng disagreed increasingly on how to pursue economic development, a conflict that intensified as the aging Mao worried about China's future after his death. When the disagreement began is unclear. Deng seems to have supported the Great Leap Forward of 1958-1959, Mao's radical approach to social and economic change, in part because it allowed the Party organization to encroach on the government administration's management of the economy. But the failure of the Great Leap and subsequent economic dislocations converted Deng to a more conservative, bureaucratic approach which deemphasized ideological exhortation and encouraged educational and scientific expertise. In contrast, Mao placed greater, though not exclusive, emphasis on minimizing elitism and on strengthening nonmaterial incentives.

Deng's change of heart made him a natural ally of Liu Shaoqi, a Party bureaucrat linked in an uneasy partnership with Mao since the 1940s and his designated heir-apparent. It is not inconceivable that Deng was positioning himself to be Liu's ultimate successor. Whatever the case, the two guided the retrenchment from the Great Leap during the early 1960s by convening a series of national conferences and promulgating pragmatic regulations. Their goal was increased production and a rationalized economic structure; but their means were not always ideologically "pure." Thus to justify a cutback of collective farming as a way of increasing food supplies, Deng asserted: "What does it matter if cats are black or white? As long as they catch mice, they are good cats."

To Mao it mattered very much whether a cat was black or white. He feared that the Liu-Deng program emphasizing economic growth and expertise would create a self-replicating elite of administrators and technocrats, thus deepening an apparent division between the Communist Party and the people. On a more personal level, Mao resented his exclusion from affairs of state by Liu and Deng (even though the Chairman had formally withdrawn from day-to-day policymaking in 1959). At a Party meeting in 1961, Mao criticized Deng for making independent decisions by asking, "Which emperor decided this?" He later complained that Deng and Liu had treated him "like a dead ancestor," that Deng "never came to consult me."

Mao's revenge came in the late 1960s when he

used his own personal prestige and the Red Guard movement to overwhelm the Party bureaucracy in the "Great Proletarian Cultural Revolution." Youthful Red Guards humiliated veterans of the Revolution. Liu Shaoqi was labeled the "Number One person in authority taking the capitalist road." Deng Xiaoping was named Number Two.

DENG THE POLITICAL PHOENIX (1966-1980)

Deng has spent many of the last years of his career trying to regain the power he lost in 1966. At the outset of the Cultural Revolution, he tried to defend himself and the Party bureaucracy against Mao and the Red Guards. But soon the tide shifted and Deng made a self-criticism:

> In retrospect, my last few years have been marked by a steady regression and due to my laxity in the study and use of Mao Tsetung [sic] Thought, I have made a number of mistakes. . . . As a result, I have become accustomed to lording it over others and acting like someone special, rarely going down among the people. . . . Worse yet still is that I have rarely reported to and asked advice from the Chairman [i.e. Mao] . . . [and] it was inevitable that I would commit an error involving political line.[13]

Late in 1966, he was driven through the streets of Beijing in a jeep, wearing a dunce-cap. He was vilified in the press and at rallies for alleged political errors ("heinous crimes"), personality faults (overconfidence and arrogance), and dissolute habits (gluttony and addiction to bridge and Mah-Jongg). Deng later disclosed that he spent the next few years in Jiangxi province. His family also suffered: his brothers were purged from their provincial level positions, and his son, Deng Bufang, was permanently crippled in an assault by Red Guards.

The Cultural Revolution devastated more than individual careers. The economy was disrupted, military officers dominated the civilian hierarchy, China's relations with other countries deteriorated, and the victors fell to fighting amongst themselves. Thus Mao, Zhou Enlai, and others had growing doubts about the loyalty of Lin Biao, minister of national defense and Mao's heir-apparent. This conflict climaxed in September 1971 when Lin's alleged plot to assassinate Mao was exposed and his escape attempt ended in a plane crash in Mongolia.

Lin's demise evidently paved the way for Deng Xiaoping's return. Mao and Zhou Enlai needed all the political help they could muster, so Zhou facilitated Deng's restoration as a vice premier of the government in April 1973. As if on trial, Deng was quite tentative during his first months back, deferring to other officials and lacking his old self-confidence. At the Tenth Party Congress in August 1973, he was restored only to the Central Committee. But he reentered the ruling Politburo late that year, after enhancing resurgent Party authority by engineering a rotation of entrenched regional military commanders. Deng also took on a new role in world affairs, traveling to both Paris and New York, where he spoke at a special session of the United Nations in 1974.

Zhou Enlai and his pragmatic colleagues had good reasons to return Deng to the top. Zhou was dying from cancer and entered the hospital in May 1974, appearing in public only a few times thereafter. He wanted a successor who supported his policies on economic growth and technical expertise and who could mobilize Party, government, and army behind them. Deng himself was apparently deeply moved by the economic devastation caused by the Cultural Revolution. The story is told of a visit Deng paid to his native Sichuan during this period. An audience that came to hear him deliver an official speech witnessed instead a unique event -- a prominent Party leader weeping, overcome with emotion. "I knew that Szechwan [sic] had suffered much," Deng reportedly said, "but only now do I realize the extent of the misery, ruin and destruction which you have experienced. I beg the people of Szechwan to forgive me for having been unable to alleviate their suffering."[14]

But Mao Zedong's highest priority was preserving a political tension between left and right. Thus he fostered the more populist and egalitarian forces around his wife (Jiang Qing) and several other radical figures (later dubbed the "gang of four"). They used their influence over the mass media to mount a series of propaganda campaigns against their more moderate opponents, led by Zhou Enlai and Deng Xiaoping, proclaiming, "We would prefer a poor society under socialism to a rich society under capitalism."

The moderates won the first round, at the Fourth National People's Congress in January 1975.

Zhou announced, and the Congress endorsed, the policy of the "four modernizations" -- of industry,
agriculture, science and technology, and national
defense -- all designed to make China an advanced
country by the year 2000. At the same time, Deng
solidified his political position: he was named
first vice premier of the government, a vice chairman of the Party, and chief-of-staff of the military. It was later revealed that he also took over
the day-to-day work of the Party Central Committee,
due to Zhou's deteriorating condition. The radicals, however, criticized the social inequalities
that rapid modernization would engender. Nonetheless, the best they could do was get Zhang Chunqiao, a principal ally of Madame Mao, named as
Deng's subordinate in the Party, government, and
military hierarchies. Mao, apparently, was not
totally satisfied with the Congress but he was not
powerful enough to challenge it.

During 1975, Deng sought to accumulate as much
power as he could before the inevitable showdown
with radicals once Zhou and Mao died. He tried to
rehabilitate as many pre-Cultural Revolution associates as possible. As in the early 1960s, he and
his subordinates drafted regulations and convened
conferences to try to lock in changes in policy.
He strengthened personal alliances, especially with
senior military officers.

But the radicals went on the offensive again
in late 1975, criticizing the moderates' proposals
for a more rigorous educational system. The attacks mounted after Zhou Enlai's death on January
8, 1976. Although Deng gave the eulogy at the memorial service for Zhou, he quickly disappeared
from public view and was labeled "an unrepentant
capitalist roader" in the radical press. In February, Mao proposed that Hua Guofeng, rather than
Deng, become acting premier.

After two months of sparring, large crowds
gathered in Zhou's memory in Beijing's Tiananmen
Square and other cities. It is said that the Beijing mourners strung small bottles from trees as a
subtle sign of support for Deng (the Chinese for
"small bottle" is the same sound as Deng's given
name). Thus challenged, the radicals had the memorial wreaths removed, aggravating the demonstration. Violence ensued, public security forces
were called in, and the radicals used the incident
to get rid of Deng. Charging him as the instigator
of a "counterrevolutionary" act, they persuaded Mao
to dismiss him from all his posts. Deng's support-

ers were strong enough to preserve his membership in the Party.

At some risk to his life, Deng left Beijing in late spring 1976 and went to Guangdong province where long-time associates protected him. We do not know Deng's precise role after being purged, but some unconfirmed reports suggest he sought the secret support of major military figures, including Defense Minister Ye Jianying, for a coup against the radicals. We do know that in October 1976, one month after Mao died, Hua Guofeng, Ye Jianying, and Wang Dongxing (Mao's former body guard) moved rapidly to arrest the leading radicals, the most prominent of whom were dubbed the "gang of four." The Politburo named Hua Party Chairman, and reinstated Zhou's "four modernizations" as central policy.

The stage was now set for Deng's second rehabilitation, but there was obvious debate within the Politburo over the terms. Some leaders, those with ties to the "gang of four" and other past opponents of Deng, apparently wanted to protect themselves against revenge and a complete political reversal. At their insistence, it seems, Deng renounced any ambition of replacing Hua Guofeng as Party chairman and endorsed the Thought of Mao Zedong (but he did not commit himself to specific principles). In addition, Deng admitted that during 1975 he had made "mistakes" (as opposed to an error in fundamental principles ["line"]). Deng's deeper regret seems to have been that he allowed the "gang" to outmaneuver him: "Because I did not do a good job in the struggle, they knocked me down."[15] As part of the bargain, he was absolved of complicity in the Tiananmen Incident (which was later relabeled a "revolutionary" act). Finally, in July 1977, he was restored to all the posts he held at the time of his purge.

But it was one thing for Deng to return to the leadership and quite another to establish his preeminence. At the time, the Politburo was evenly divided between older veterans of the revolution and relatively younger officials, many of whom had benefited from the Cultural Revolution. While the latter group did not necessarily favor a return to the policies advocated by the radicals in the mid-1970s, they did oppose policy experiments that violated what they held as the fundamental tenets of Maoism. Deng believed that modernization could not succeed if those limits remained, and he worked persistently and methodically to remove them. In a series of intense political struggles, he and his

associates kept up the pressure on their opponents.
Each time the conflict came to a head, Deng seems
to have won less than he wanted. On at least one
occasion, he was the object of a vigorous counter-
attack. But each time he regrouped his forces, executed a variety of maneuvers to further isolate
his opponents, and then pressed his advantage.
Over the long term, he has accomplished much more
than most observers expected.

Deng has used a three-pronged strategy in this
complex political struggle (about which subsequent
chapters provide additional detail).   The first
prong is ridding the political sphere of the Maoist
legacy. A decisive victory in the political arena
was essential if the bureaucracy and the people at
large were to be confident that Deng's approach to
modernization would continue after his death.   The
political battle was waged on several fronts.   To
create more consensus in the ruling Politburo, Deng
and his allies brought in new members who shared
their views and weakened those who did not, either
by denying them an administrative power or by re-
moving them entirely. To legitimize his program,
Deng has gained an increasingly explicit repudiation of the Cultural Revolution and the man who
started it, by rehabilitating most of its victims
and by attacking the dogmatism associated with it.
For a time in late 1978, he relaxed the controls on
popular expression to build support for his attack
on Mao and for his own policies.   Deng has also
moved to lock in those policies by engineering the
rapid rise of two proteges -- Zhao Ziyang, who is
now the leading figure in the state administration,
and Hu Yaobang, who sits atop the Party apparatus.

Much of Deng's activity has been at the expense of Chairman and Premier Hua Guofeng, Mao's
chosen successor.   Hua has certainly participated
in the emerging collective leadership and has
served as the titular figure in China's foreign
relations.   How much power he has now and how much
he will be able to accumulate in the years ahead is
uncertain.

The second element of Deng's strategy is fostering greater autonomy for a broad range of social
institutions, and by implication, altering their
relationship with the political structure. Modernization, it is believed, depends on an increased
role -- in economic management, science, education,
and law -- for experts immune from excessive political interference.   In other areas -- the arts,
personal lifestyles, and religion -- a relaxation

of political controls will encourage people to more
actively support the modernization drive.

Third, Deng has reemphasized and extended the
internationalist strain of Chinese Communism. He
has continued the foreign policy pursued by Mao and
Zhou Enlai in the 1970s -- oppose the Soviet Union
by allying with its enemies -- but has been more
willing to compromise on past principles. The December 1978 agreement with the United States on
normalization of diplomatic relations is only the
most prominent example.

Deng's opening to the outside world was motivated by more than geopolitics. The advanced
industrial world serves two other purposes --
shocking Chinese into a realization of how backward
their society is economically, and providing the
technology to overcome that backwardness. Thus
Deng has encouraged countless visits by central and
provincial officials to visit foreign countries,
and his own trips to Japan (October 1978) and the
United States (January-February 1979) received extensive media coverage in China. To speed China's
technological revolution, Deng has launched inno-
vations in foreign trade and investment that were
unthinkable during the Maoist era.

Nonetheless, that era is still too recent and
its principles are still accorded too much respect
for Deng to escape without criticism. Especially in
the spring of 1979, the consequences of many of his
controversial policies provided those with Maoist
inclinations a pretext for attacking him. The expansion of political expression had led to attacks
on the system itself and to social disorder. The
emphasis on China's backwardness offended the Chinese sense of national pride, and some were critical of the invasion of Vietnam in February 1979.
Ambitious capital construction plans were found
wanting when compared to China's ability to implement them.

Aside from providing Deng's opponents with a
political opportunity, these problems also bothered
individuals who were usually his allies. Deng
therefore tacked into the winds of opposition to
accommodate their concerns. The ambitious economic
plans were cut back. The conditions under which
individuals and social institutions exercise autonomy were clarified, especially in the area of political expression. Then, having consolidated his
position, Deng continued his political assault
through early 1980.

The early 1979 setback exemplifies what will

be a continuing problem for Deng. He is trying to reshape the most populous society in the world, with only limited resources at his disposal. He has begun to lay the foundation for his own succession, but history has shown the limits of what any leader can do in that regard. To implement his programs, he must work through a bureaucracy that is protective of its manifold vested interests. The sacrifice and commitment of the population at large is essential, but disappointed expectations or cynicism are already problems. Economic growth is dependent on a host of unknowns, including the weather, the extent of China's extractable oil reserves, and the state of the international economy. The early 1980s will be a key testing period for Deng's approach to modernization and his political skill in guaranteeing its survival after his death. The results of that test will shape China's long-term future.

CONCLUSION

Intelligence, arrogance, persistence, ambition -- these are some of the personal qualities that propelled Deng to the vanguard of the Chinese Communist movement. But let us conclude this portrait by noting his three most prominent political characteristics, which twice gave his rivals cause to send him to the rear guard:

--although pragmatic, he is a Marxist. He is willing to appeal to private interests and extend material incentives. But he believes firmly that socialism (the primacy of public ownership of production and of economic planning) is the only road for China. He belongs to the school of Chinese Marxism that emphasizes the building of a technological and human base, even though that may risk growing inequality.
--although outward looking, he remains a staunch Chinese nationalist. Unlike some of his rivals, he believes China must open up to advanced foreign science and technology, even at the risk of some exposure to "bourgeois" values. But Deng sees this modernization approach leading to a strong, more prosperous, and secure China. In his view, "self-reliance" is contingent upon, not opposed to, "learning from advanced countries."
--although he is not a Maoist, he remains a revolutionary. Though he abhors mass movements, he advocates rapid change in every sector of Chinese

society, implemented by a competent and reliable political structure. In that sense, he too is a "radical."

NOTES

1.   Foreign Broadcast Information Service, Daily Report: People's Republic of China, 11 March 1980, Supplement (hereafter referred to as "FBIS Supplement"), p. 1.   Various unofficial versions of Deng's speech have appeared; this translation is based on one that appeared in the Hong Kong Communist monthly Cheng Ming, no. 29 (March 1980):11-23. This introductory section is based on Deng's speech and a contemporaneous article, "Why China Has Opened its Doors," that Deng wrote for the Bangkok Post of February 10, 1980, translated in FBIS, Daily Report: People's Republic of China, 12 February 1980, pp. Ll - L5.
2.   "Why China Has Opened its Doors," p. Ll.
3.   FBIS Supplement, p. 17.
4.   "Why China Has Opened its Doors," p. L2; FBIS Supplement, p. 19.
5.   "Why China Has Opened its Doors," p. L3.
6.   FBIS Supplement, p. 23.
7.   FBIS Supplement, p. 11.
8.   "Teng's Speech to the Third Plenum, July 1977," reprinted in translation in Contemporary China 2, no. 1 (Spring 1978):176.
9.   Roderick MacFarquahar, The Origins of the Cultural Revolution: Contradictions Among the People 1956-1957 (New York: Columbia University Press, 1974), p. 142.
10. MacFarquahar, Origins, p. 142.
11. "Speech to the Third Plenum," p. 178.
12. William W. Whitson, The Chinese High Command: A History of Communist Military Politics (New York: Praeger, 1973), p. 158.
13. Chi Hsin, Teng Hsiao-ping -- a political biography (Hong Kong: Cosmos Books, 1978), pp. 62-64.
14. Miriam London and Ivan D. London, "Hunger in China: The 'Norm of Truth,'" Worldview 22, no. 3 (1979):13-14.
15. "Speech to the Third Plenum," p. 179.

3
Politics in the PRC:
Entering the Fourth Decade

David M. Lampton

INTRODUCTION

Mao Zedong died in September 1976. By early 1980, it appeared that his attempt during his waning years to infuse China with egalitarian values might be dead as well. Especially since late 1978, Mao's opponents from the Cultural Revolution decade (1966-1976) have won a series of major political victories which amount to a stinging repudiation of the late Party Chairman's rule. Led by Vice Premier Deng Xiaoping, the present leadership has:

--purged most of Mao's Cultural Revolution allies;
--rehabilitated almost all of Mao's ardent critics and adversaries;
--abandoned the Maoist value of equality in the formulation of economic and social policy, replacing it with equity in order to spur rapid economic growth;
--implied that Mao died twenty years too late, and that he left China awash in political instability, low economic productivity, and public cynicism.

All that is missing is explicit condemnation of the man who dominated that country for nearly thirty years.

But repudiating Mao himself does not eradicate the problems he is said to have left behind. To deal with the problem of political instability, the new leadership has restored to power victims of the Cultural Revolution who had been prominent in the 1950s and early 1960s. But can men in their seven-

25

ties and eighties lead China towards the twenty-
first century? Can they mobilize the enthusiasm of
the younger officials whose career advancement has
been slowed?

For China to solve its economic and social
problems, Deng and his colleagues are recommending
innovation ("emancipate the mind"). But will a
bureaucratic system devoted to protecting its
prerogatives and inclined to centralization be
willing to relax its control in order to stimulate
innovation?

Finally, any regime cultivates political support by establishing a shared sense of justice, a
legitimate basis for the exercise of authority and
the resolution of conflict. But during the past
fifteen years of political turmoil, various leaders
at all levels have meted out their own version of
justice. Can the current leadership rebuild popular confidence in the regime? Can it put to rest
the fears that the state will continue to regard
policy differences as intolerable dissent? In
short, has the political system itself become an
obstacle to solving China's problems? As China
enters its fourth decade under Communist rule, the
leaders in Beijing are seeking to prove that this
is not the case.

BURYING THE CULTURAL REVOLUTION WITH MAO: TRYING TO ACHIEVE STABILITY AND UNITY

Mao began the Cultural Revolution to stop
"revisionism" -- the emergence, in his eyes, of a
bureaucratic elite divorced from the people and
pursuing policies that resulted in inequalities in
wealth and status.

During 1977 and 1978, it became progressively
clear to Deng Xiaoping and his colleagues that they
would have to attack the Cultural Revolution and
its ideological underpinnings because they were
obstacles to rapid economic growth. Even as late
as 1978, many cadres at the middle and lower
reaches of the administrative apparatus saw little
reason to commit themselves fully to the modernization policies. In fact, there were good reasons
to stand pat.

Several of Mao's Cultural Revolution allies,
still in their fifties and sixties, remained on the
Party's ruling Politburo. The pragmatists in
charge were generally in their seventies. How long
would the latter group be around to protect their
supporters from a comeback by the former?

In addition, about one-half the Party's 38 million members, difficult enough to control in the best of times, had joined during the Cultural Revolution decade, stirred by slogans like "never forget class struggle" and "it is right to rebel." Indeed, many had gained their positions by attacking older officials. By late 1978, the pragmatic course in economic, social, and foreign policies was having an unsettling effect on the Party. Party members who had risen by virtue of their zealous pursuit of Cultural Revolution values were now implementing policies inconsistent with those values. Others were simply afraid that the political winds would shift again, leaving them vulnerable. As some cadres in the central province of Henan put it: "We are now doing things which we criticized in the past and criticizing things which we did in the past; we feel really confused." Could that kind of "lingering fear" be ended by anything less than a root and branch rejection of the theoretical justification of the Cultural Revolution (the danger of "revisionism")?

Thus from late 1978 to early 1980, Deng and his colleagues stepped up their attack on the Cultural Revolution's ideology and beneficiaries. On the ideological front, the third plenary session of the Eleventh Central Committee of the Party (December 1978) acknowledged that there had been "shortcomings and mistakes" in the Cultural Revolution. On the occasion of the thirtieth anniversary of the founding of the People's Republic (October 1979) Party elder and Vice Chairman Ye Jianying went further: he rejected Mao's definition of revisionism and said that the Cultural Revolution had "embodied an erroneous policy and method of struggle. . . ." The process climaxed at the Central Committee's fifth plenum (February 1980). The meeting restored the "good name" of the late Liu Shaoqi -- Mao's principal target in the Cultural Revolution -- and renounced a 1968 designation of Liu as a "scab, hidden renegade, and traitor to the Chinese revolution." The persecution that Liu suffered at the hands of Mao was said to have been an error.

For Deng and his allies, it was not enough to deal with the Cultural Revolution on an ideological level. They reinforced their attack with changes in the leadership. At the third plenum, four Deng supporters (Chen Yun, Wang Zhen, Hu Yaobang, and Deng Yingchao [Mme. Zhou Enlai]) were added to the Politburo. Four Maoist holdovers -- Wang Dongxing, Chen Xilian, Wu De, and Ji Dengkui -- relinquished

Hu Yaobang (Eastfoto)

Zhao Ziyang (Eastfoto)

some of their administrative posts. In June 1979, three consistent critics of Mao's approach to the economy -- Chen Yun, Bo Yibo, and Yao Yilin -- became vice premiers in the government structure. In September 1979, Peng Zhen, the first major victim of the Cultural Revolution, returned to the Politburo. And in February 1980, the four Maoist holdouts -- Wang, Chen, Wu, and Ji -- were removed from the Politburo while two close associates of Deng -- Hu Yaobang and Zhao Ziyang -- joined its standing committee.

Simultaneous with these changes at the top, there has been a "reversal of verdicts" throughout the Party structure. Those purged from official posts during the Cultural Revolution were entitled to have their previous positions restored if still alive. If dead, blots on their record were removed. Memorial services for those who had died as a result of "persecution by Lin Biao and the gang of four" were a constant feature all over China throughout 1979. By early 1980, almost every major figure (living and dead) who had run afoul of Mao and his associates since 1959 had been rehabilitated.

Ironically, the effort to rectify past wrongs and enhance leadership consensus has created new problems. Politburo changes have left the Party elite older than ever. The average age of Politburo members is now over seventy. Further down the hierarchy, old cadres hold major positions but are too infirm to perform their duties. The Chinese press has frankly acknowledged that "the universal lack of young and vigorous middle-aged and young cadres among leading bodies at various levels represents an even more serious problem. . . . Some veteran cadres cannot even maintain eight hours of work." It appears that the Party will try to deal with this vexing problem as it revises its constitution. Until there is an effective retirement system, younger officials will be blocked from playing a vigorous and innovative role.

The "reversal of verdicts" has created a host of concrete problems for local leaders. Since late 1978, petitioners have besieged local governments demanding that wrongs suffered during the Cultural Revolution be rectified, that they receive compensation for (or restitution of) confiscated property, that they receive back pay, and that erroneous class labels be altered. The situation in Shanghai suggests the dimension of the problem. In late 1979, the authorities reported that "during the ten

years of the . . . Cultural Revolution there were
more than 220,000 cases in Shanghai in which people
were wronged, misjudged, or framed. . . . As of
now, more than 90 percent of the cases . . . have
been reviewed with many frame-ups and wrong cases
redressed. In addition, those who were wrongly
persecuted to death have been exonerated." The regime has dispatched special teams to review the
mountain of cases. Yet by their nature many of the
grievances can never be assuaged.

The youth problem has been another source of
urban instability. From 1966 to 1976, large cities
in China, particularly Shanghai, were "drained" of
young persons. Shanghai sent as many as one million high school graduates, somewhat less than ten
percent of its population, to the countryside.
Those "sent down" now want to return to the cities
to take advantage of the new emphasis on education
and urban employment. As the lure of urban lights
increases, many young people have returned illegal-
ly, producing inevitable conflicts with local
authorities. In Shanghai in early 1979, for example, groups of youths disrupted transportation,
government offices, and various services to press
their demand to stay in the city.

In response, the authorities have used both
the stick and the carrot. There has been a crack-
down on delinquency and crime (some returned youth
have resorted to petty theft to survive). On the
other hand, Chinese leaders have promised that the
flow of young people to the cities will grow as the
urban economy expands. To accelerate the expansion
of the urban job market, the regime has allowed
some youth to form "profit and loss" service coop-
eratives. And some attempts have been made to
improve conditions for those who have to remain
down on the farm. Despite these measures, the
youth problem remains serious, and its solution
awaits a broad, sustained economic advance.

FROM EQUALITY TO EQUITY: BEIJING'S ATTEMPT TO ACCELERATE ECONOMIC GROWTH

Since 1949, leaders in Beijing have repeatedly
debated how to distribute scarce material goods and
services. The debate centers on the values of
"equality" and "equity," each having very different
effects on social welfare and labor productivity.
An equality-based distributive policy allocates
goods and services to all regardless of effort.
Equity-based distribution emphasizes an individ-

uals's contribution to a given social objective.

It would be overstating the case to say that
Mao's China pursued egalitarian policies exclusively, or that all such policies have disappeared.
Since late 1978 nonetheless, there has been a
decided swing toward equity. Those who make the
greatest contribution to growth and "modernization," it is now stridently proclaimed, will
receive income and social services in greatest
abundance. For those who are a drag on the economy, there may be sanctions. Policies designed to
heighten equity will increase inequalities among
individuals, among villages, counties, and provinces, and between urban and rural areas along a
number of dimensions. Although the state has taken
special measures to raise rural incomes, it still
seems that urban life will appear more and more
attractive.

Concerning income distribution, Beijing has
enunciated a crisp doctrine -- the more one works,
the more one gets. In March 1979, the leading
Party theoretical journal stated: "Some people
will be first to receive a larger income and live a
better life. Such a situation will encourage or
stimulate others to contribute more to the state."

Payment systems have changed in support of
this doctrine. Household income is determined
primarily by the quantity, skill, and vigor of a
family's labor power. Task-rate (i.e. quota)
systems allow families with more labor power to
reap the full benefits of their advantage, while
time-rate schemes mute differences and produce
fewer inequalities. Whereas time-rate systems were
common during much of the 1970s, task-rate systems
have received increasing attention since late 1978,
with the inevitable effect on income inequality.
Similarly, a new system of job contracting in rural
areas in which payment is based on output will
benefit vigorous and well located groups.

Changes in state investment in both agriculture and industry are increasing the already-siz-
able economic gaps among communes, counties, and
provinces. Concerning the rural sector, Beijing
declared in spring 1979 that it would concentrate
investment in "high and stable yield areas," that
is, those areas that are already most productive.
They will become even more productive, and people
within them will become relatively more prosperous.

In industry, the current leadership is altering the long-standing policy of equalizing industrial investment among all provinces. In early

1979, economic planners openly questioned the wisdom of this policy, saying that previous investment in poor, backward, and isolated areas had frequently been wasteful. In apparent support, Party Chairman Hua Guofeng noted in a major speech that "Twenty-four percent of our state industrial enterprises are run at varying degrees of loss." By the end of 1979, over 2,000 plants had closed because of their inefficiencies. Now substantial investment funds will be distributed through banks in the form of loans. Areas most able to repay the loans will be the first to receive credit, a practice which will work to the detriment of weaker enterprises and poorer provinces.

In medical care, equality has been downplayed once again. The regime has seemingly set aside Mao's 1965 dictum to "put the stress on the rural areas." This doctrine had sparked dramatic reforms in rural health care delivery and medical education but also produced a deterioration in urban health services. In 1979, leaders in the health field boldly called for "modernization" of one-third of the country's hospitals by 1985. The minister of public health said that "Modernization requires people versed in modern science and techniques, equipment for hospitals and research institutes, and scientific management of the medical system." As urban health has received more attention, the emphasis given rural medicine declines. Whether that will be reflected in actual services delivered remains to be seen.

Population control is now subject to the principle of equity, since providing services for excessive numbers of children depletes investment funds. In August 1979, Vice Premier Chen Muhua announced tough new policies regarding family size. The guidelines encouraged couples to have one child (as opposed to two as before). Such families would receive food, clothing, and housing as though they had two children. Families with two children would receive neither rewards nor sanctions, but couples who had a third child would suffer various penalties (denial of additional rations was an oft-mentioned sanction). As Chen wrote in August, "People who refuse to be persuaded and insist on having more children will be taxed." How does this approach affect existing inequalities? By all accounts, the birth rate in rural areas is substantially higher than in the city. If rigorously enforced, the new policy will impose sanctions disproportionately on peasants, on those already at a lower economic level, and on those who believe that they have the greatest economic need for children.

To summarize, there has been a striking shift away from equality since late 1978. The new touchstone for policy is equity: those individuals, families, units, and provinces that contribute most to economic growth will receive the greatest rewards. But pursuing equity could be politically explosive if the economy does not grow fast enough to provide benefits for all. For instance, a coalition of have-nots is conceivable -- provinces with declining investment funds, villages getting a smaller piece of the pie, workers discharged from inefficient factories, and peasants whose social services lag behind those of their city cousins. Such a coalition might find Mao's vision of growth <u>with</u> equality very attractive. Whether it would get support from segments of the bureaucracy or leadership is a critical unknown.

WINNING POPULAR SUPPORT AND REBUILDING A STRUCTURE FOR PARTICIPATION

The turmoil of the Cultural Revolution decade gravely eroded popular support for the Communist regime, especially in the cities. Mounting cynicism greeted each new power struggle and policy shift. Professionals and intellectuals, primary targets of Maoist Red Guards, were only willing to go through the motions, except in the most politically secure fields. Political didacticism in the arts left a cultural desert. The legal system, such as it was prior to 1966, had been destroyed. Non-elective revolutionary committees replaced nominally elective people's governments. Personal expression was risky at best.

Since Mao's death, and especially since late 1978, the regime has tried in a variety of ways to restore some semblance of a popular mandate. They have attempted to do so by restoring excluded groups to an active role and by recreating a stable set of expectations for relations between the government and the people.

Through "united front work," the Communist Party has tried to win the cooperation and involvement of non-Communist groups, and the united front policy of 1978-1979 was not unlike that of previous periods of relaxation. The package included: encouraging popular expression ("let a hundred flowers bloom and a hundred schools of thought contend"), recruiting Party members among intellectuals and professionals, improving the working conditions of scientists, and reducing Party control over research. Scientists especially have enjoyed a new prominence due to their centrality to the modernization drive.

The regime has also sought recently to rekindle creativity and commitment among China's writers and artists, who had been under assault throughout the Cultural Revolution. A conference of writers and artists, convened in Beijing in October-November 1979, brought together victims of Maoist cultural policies dating back to the pre-1949 period. Speakers called on those assembled to employ a diversity of stylistic techniques and to range widely in picking subjects. Party bureaucrats were instructed to "respect the experts."

Along with the return of scientists, writers, artists, and other professionals, Deng and his colleagues have tried to rebuild a political and legal structure. Revolutionary committees -- the local government institutions of the Cultural Revolution -- were abolished. In their place came people's governments and people's congresses, whose organization and functions were codified in new laws. Delegates to congresses up to the county level were to be selected by direct election, with candidates outnumbering positions to be filled. By late 1979, elections had begun in selected localities, and are scheduled to continue throughout the country over the course of 1980. There were other signs of expanding political participation -- such as "opinion polls" to select workshop heads in factories, and the dropping of "class background" as a criterion for political activity, recruitment, and promotion.

At the same time, there has been an effort to make the criminal justice system more predictable. In June 1979, the regime unveiled a criminal code, standards of criminal procedure, and statutes governing the court system and procuracy. After several months of public education and discussion, these went into effect on January 1, 1979.

But the wall poster campaign that commenced in Beijing in late 1978 had by the end of 1979 become a nagging challenge to the new political and legal structure. Initially, Deng and his allies in the national leadership tolerated, and in some cases encouraged, the display of "big character posters" on "democracy walls" in the capital and elsewhere. But soon, posters became highly critical of the regime and on occasion called for fundamental change in the political system. Others criticized China's February 1979 invasion of Vietnam. The "Beijing spring" ended as Wei Jingsheng, editor of a dissident tabloid, was arrested, and poster substance and location were restricted.

Wei Jingsheng came to trial in the fall, charged with transmitting "state secrets" to foreigners and purveying "counterrevolutionary propaganda." Wei based his defense on the section of China's constitution guaranteeing the right of free speech, and pointed out that all the information he had disseminated was already public knowledge. He went further, stating, in a tone not calculated to win the hearts of prosecutors, "The central theme in my articles . . . is that without democracy there will be no four modernizations." Despite the prosecution's clumsy handling of the case, Wei received a predictably long sentence (Deng Xiaoping asserted that it was "necessary to set an example"). The reaction from the West was sharp, and the US government protested the sentence. In February 1980, the Party forbade the public display of posters entirely, in order to prevent people like Wei Jingsheng from emerging in the future.

The Wei Jingsheng case and the restriction of public expression raise a number of serious questions bearing on the general effort to regain popular support. In the wake of Wei's case, how much trust will the new legal system inspire in China, where the roots of legal codes are shallow and those of authoritarianism are deep? Do people in China, like some abroad, believe that Deng manipulated the free speech movement for his own ends, turning on the posters to discredit his opponents and turning them off when that purpose had been achieved? If so, can they take seriously the regime's support for "socialist democracy"? Will professionals and intellectuals be willing to speak their minds?

It also remains to be seen what consequences these moves will have for the Party and the bureaucracy. It is possible that recruiting more professionals and intellectuals into the Party will bring them into closer conflict with the very cadres who attacked and replaced them during the Cultural Revolution. If the Party becomes the principal avenue of professional mobility, it may become less and less responsive to the needs of those at the bottom of the social and economic ladder. At a deeper

level, the elite faces a dilemma. It seemingly
wants the benefits of a liberalized cultural and
legal system without bearing the inevitable costs.
It wants innovation and creativity, but only that
which does not threaten its control. It wants "law
above men," but only as long as it does not threat-
en those at the top. A question for the future is:
will the current liberalization expand and deepen
over time, or will it frighten the bureaucracy to
such an extent that it treats the present set of
policies as just another tactical move, to be
abandoned as soon as its interests are no longer
served?

PROBLEMS AND PROSPECTS FOR THE FUTURE

Leadership, social stability, economic growth,
and securing a popular mandate have been high on
the Chinese political agenda since Mao's death. As
the leadership in Beijing enters the 1980s, it
clearly recognizes that younger leaders at all
levels must be groomed for leadership, that employment and a sense of self-worth must be provided to
China's youth, and that intellectuals and professionals must be induced to play a positive role in
China's development. However, to diagnose a dis-
ease is not to cure it, and profound difficulties
lie ahead. First of all, how can the regime
distribute the inevitable burdens and benefits of
modernization in a way that is perceived to be
"fair"? Will backward provinces, isolated peasants, workers in small plants, and the "lost generation" of Cultural Revolution youth accept as
"just" the present and future distribution of
benefits? Some must still harbor a faith in Mao's
Cultural Revolution ideology, based as it was on
equality.
Secondly, China's need to promote young leaders has run head-on into the policy of righting the
wrongs of the Cultural Revolution and thus reward-
ing age. In the midst of loud and repeated calls
for promoting younger persons, countless younger
Party members have to step aside in favor of older
ones. Can and will the Party authorities not only
talk about cultivating younger leaders but in fact
start giving them some responsiblity? Will this
happen before the actuarial tables catch up with
China's aging gerontocracy?
Finally, slow economic growth or stagnation
will aggravate social and leadership conflicts.
Will there be sufficient capital to modernize agri-

culture, build basic infrastructure, and develop petroleum and other mineral extraction? Will the investment produce the anticipated returns? On the other side of the coin, can China reduce its population growth rate enough to provide economic breathing space? Officials have predicted a population of four billion persons by 2080 if every woman of childbearing age were to have three children. To China's leadership, this is a spectre of truly frightening proportions.

As Deng Xiaoping and his colleagues enter the 1980's, they face an imposing challenge: delivering enough benefits to enough people to justify having abandoned Mao's vision of growth with equality. Because the changes needed to make China more prosperous and modern will be painful to literally millions of people, meeting that challenge will not be easy. But if the new leadership fails to achieve rapid and sustained growth, it may find it difficult to keep Mao buried.

4
China's Economic Readjustment: Recovery or Paralysis?

Nicholas R. Lardy

INTRODUCTION

During the winter of 1978-1979, China's leaders undertook a profound reappraisal of the Chinese
economy -- its successes, failures, and future
prospects. By the end of this period, they had
discarded the widely heralded Ten Year Economic
Plan (1976-1985), which was only formally unveiled
in February 1978.* In its place, they adopted a
drastically revised set of developmental policies,
designed to cope with problems not usually associated with China: unemployment, declining housing
standards, and hunger. The new "readjustment" approach, which curtails the rate of investment and
raises the priority of agriculture, light industry,
and housing, has proved initially successful in al-
leviating some of these difficulties. Nonetheless,
at the end of 1979 there appeared to to be sharp
divisions within China concerning the objectives of
economic development policy. Critics of the new
approach have used its initial success to argue
that further reductions in the rate of investment
slated for the annual plan for 1980 are unneces-
sary, and that the three-year readjustment period
should be truncated. This policy dispute is perceived only dimly outside of China, but it seems
not impossible that division and indecision over

---

*China's leadership had begun consideration of
the Ten Year Plan in 1975, but discussion soon
stopped, amid the political turmoil preceding the
death of Mao Zedong in September 1976. After the
purge of the "gang of four" one month later, it
still took over a year to work out even general
priorities.

resource allocation could lead, as in the past, to a period of somewhat curtailed growth.

THE SHIFT IN PRIORITIES

The abandonment of the Ten Year Plan and its replacement with a revised economic policy under the slogan of "readjustment, restructuring, consolidation, and improvement" became official at the second session of the Fifth National People's Congress in June 1979. The Ten Year Plan, which had been endorsed by the Fifth Congress' first session in February 1978, was formally replaced with a three-year period of readjustment, and a subsequent Sixth Five Year Plan (1981-1985). These changes were hardly semantic for they were predicated on a recognition that the economy was suffering from major structural problems. Furthermore, some of the ultimate goals for 1985 were sharply at variance with those initially disclosed in 1978.

The most salient element of the revised development strategy is a shift of resources away from investment and toward increased consumption. For more than two decades the state held down real wages and allocated to reinvestment a growing share of profits from its enterprises. Profits soared from 14 billion yuan in 1957 to 44 billion yuan in 1978, while investment tripled to more than 39 billion yuan during the same period. Consequently, per capita consumption expenditures have grown relatively slowly since the mid-1950s.

In 1979, Chinese planners deliberately reduced investment and raised the level of both urban and rural incomes. Two-thirds of China's urban work force received wage increases in the fall of 1977; 40 percent of the work force got further raises in late 1979. Farm incomes, too, have been rising significantly since the December 1979 decision of the third plenum of the Central Committee to raise prices paid by the state for farm products by about 25 percent. These measures were undertaken because the program's drafters believe it will be impossible to meet the expectations generated by the modernization drive and to raise labor productivity without raising the material standard of living in food, manufactured consumer goods, and housing.

Regarding food, documents of the third plenum revealed that average per capita food grain supplies were lower in 1977 than in 1957 and that more

than one hundred million Chinese had inadequate
quantities of food grains -- the basic staple of
the diet. Other data released subsequently show
that per capita supplies of fish, fats and oils,
and fruit had actually declined in the twenty years
between 1957 and 1977. Western analysts, using
Chinese agricultural production data, estimate that
average food intake in 1977 was only 2,000 calories
per person per day. The share of calories derived
from sources other than cereals, tubers, and pulses
is the lowest of any country in Asia. This reflects the scarcity of meat (average per capita
consumption 17 pounds per year), fish (12 pounds),
fruit (13 pounds), sugar (4 pounds), milk products
(less than 2 ounces), and other nongrain items.

A second area of plan revision, which is of
equal concern from the point of view of improved
incentives and labor productivity, is increased
supplies of manufactured consumer goods. These
products include a broad spectrum ranging from
bicycles, sewing machines, radios, and televisions
to sundry products of everyday use -- furniture,
clothing, etc. The textile industry, for example,
is to be developed more rapidly to increase the
available supplies of cotton clothing, which have
been rationed at a fairly constant per capita standard for almost thirty years. The new emphasis in
consumer goods is not motivated solely by welfare
considerations. For regularized wage increases and
bonuses to have their desired positive effects, the
volume, quality, and variety of manufactured goods
will have to be raised.

Finally, housing remains a pressing need of
China's urban population. Twenty-five years ago
the Chinese aimed for a standard of six square
meters of living space per capita in urban areas.
But the pace of new construction has not kept up
with the growth of the urban population. Thus,
living space in 193 large and medium size cities in
China with a population of 70 million persons is
only 3.6 square meters per capita -- actually a
decline from the area available more than twenty
years ago. At the same time, the quality of
China's inherited housing stock, particularly in
older cities, has been allowed to deteriorate.
Maintenance has been neglected because the minimal
rental fees charged by the state have generally
been inadequate to finance more than the most
superficial repairs.

Besides reducing the overall rate of investment, the "readjustment" policies call for a shift

in sectoral investment priorities. The priority
formerly assigned to steel and its supporting heavy
industry has been sharply scaled back, while relative allocations for agriculture, light industry,
housing, and infrastructure investment have increased. The initial target of 60 million tons of
steel output in 1985 has now been substantially
reduced to 45 million tons. The revisions also
recognize the need to alleviate bottlenecks in
electric power supply and transportation systems.

Agriculture's new priority is perhaps the most
significant. China has long enunciated the slogan
that "agriculture is the foundation of the economy," but this was not usually matched by the allocation of investment resources. We now know that
agriculture's share of investment resources has
been relatively small, except for a few years during the food crisis of the early 1960s. When
available, items such as machinery and chemical
fertilizers were usually low in quality and high in
price, reducing the incentive for raising farm output. But recently, state investment in agriculture
has been raised from about 10 to 15 percent of
state investment and state bank loans to agriculture have also been greatly increased. Enhanced
production incentives reinforce this shift: in the
summer of 1979 the government increased the prices
it pays peasants for agricultural products by an
average of 25 percent; the level of compulsory
deliveries is to be stabilized; and the prices for
deliveries above the quota have been raised by even
larger amounts -- 30 percent for cotton and 50 percent for grains and oils and fats.

The government, for the first time in a decade, is also encouraging peasants to capitalize on
their comparative advantage and specialize in the
food or animal products for which their natural
conditions are best suited. Assignment of compulsory sown-area targets for specific crops is being
reduced. After a ten-year hiatus, rural free markets are again being encouraged as an outlet for
peasants to sell their specialized products. Concurrently the state has stepped up its previously
curtailed efforts to guarantee adequate supplies of
basic food products to those areas that choose to
specialize in animal husbandry or in commercial
crops like cotton.

These new agricultural policies must be judged
an initial success. Food grain production has increased by more than 30 million metric tons (12
percent) since 1977. Even more marked has been the

increased output of oil-bearing crops such as rape, peanuts, and sesame (up to 50 percent in 1979 compared to 1977), and sugar. Raising the price for grain delivered to the state has had an even more dramatic effect on state procurement. The 1979 summer grain harvest exceeded that of the summer before by about 10 percent (rising to 64.9 million metric tons), but sales to the state rose by more than 40 percent, overfulfilling the planned target by a third. Similarly, deliveries of rapeseed (China's major oil-bearing crop) rose at a much faster rate than output, overfulfilling the 1979 target by more than 40 percent. Average per capita supplies of food grains have now surpassed their previous peak levels and consumption of oils, animal products, and other nonstaple foods have increased sharply in the past two years. However, per capita consumption of several nongrain food products remains below the level of the 1950s.

Meeting expectations for improved supplies of manufactured consumer goods will be much more difficult. In some product lines the productive capacity already exists, but shortages of electric power and raw materials limit the growth of output. Productivity increases are constrained by an absence of management reform. While steps have already been taken to alleviate critical bottlenecks, it will be several years before these constraints can be eased. In the short run the state gave priority to light and textile industries in the allocation of fuel, power, and raw and semifinished materials. As a result, the 1979 output of light manufactured goods surpassed the 8 percent target and, for the first time in memory, grew more rapidly than heavy industry.

Finally, improvements in urban housing are coming at an even slower pace. Because of the slow rate of construction during the 1966-1976 decade, when the average annual additions to the housing stock were less than those achieved from 1952 to 1957, the backlog of unmet needs is staggering. Policymakers have responded in two ways. To restrict demand, they continue to limit rural-urban migration, transfer some middle school graduates to the countryside, and severely limit the growth of the largest urban centers where the per unit costs of housing and other infrastructure are the highest. To increase supply, state investment in housing has increased sharply since 1977 both in absolute terms and as a share of total state investment. In a step of greater potential significance,

the state has authorized on an experimental basis
the construction of private urban housing in a few
cities. This is a sharp departure from the government's previous position as a monopoly supplier of
urban housing, but it is being tried as a means of
partially overcoming the constraints imposed by
overstretched state investment resources and the
low productivity of state construction programs.
Despite these adjustments, however, it will be several years before even the relatively low urban
housing standards of the 1950s can be attained,
even if housing continues to be put up at the
current record-breaking pace.

UNEMPLOYMENT AND INFLATION

For years China was thought to have largely
escaped two of the most vexing contemporary economic problems: unemployment and inflation. Urban
unemployment, widespread in the 1950s, had been
avoided after the late 1960s largely by resettling
up to fifteen million urban middle school graduates
in the countryside. Under the somewhat more relaxed policies of the post-Mao regime, however,
millions of these youths have returned to the
cities, hoping finally to find jobs in the modern
sector that would utilize their training. In a
speech last year, it was officially revealed that
twenty million urban residents, just over 20 percent of the urban labor force, were unemployed at
the beginning of 1979.

By the end of 1979, the Chinese press reported
that over nine million new jobs had been created,
but this is far from satisfactory for two reasons.
First, a large portion of the new jobs has probably
gone to new entrants into the urban labor market,
of which there are three million each year. Thus,
the number of unemployed workers had probably been
reduced by far less than nine million. Second,
one-half of the new jobs have come in a secondary
job market -- the so-called collective sector.
These jobs, usually in handicrafts, repair, res-
taurants, and other services, typically pay substantially less than jobs in the state sector and
do not usually provide important benefits such as
free health care and retirement pensions. Partly
as a result of the inability of the government to
provide meaningful employment to millions of
youths, urban crime has become a rapidly growing
problem in many Chinese cities.

A second cause of economic dissatisfaction in

contemporary China is inflation. For over twenty
years urban retail food prices were quite stable.
That ended in November 1979 when the government
raised prices for eight nonstaple foods (pork,
poultry, beef, mutton, eggs, vegetables, fish, and
milk) by an average of one-third. Ostensibly the
increase was a consequence of the April 1st rise in
the state procurement prices of eighteen major
agricultural products: from April until November
the state was selling products at retail prices
that were sometimes below the procurement prices it
paid to farmers. Not surprisingly, many entre-
preneurial peasants purchased quantities of non-
rationed food products such as eggs and then resold
them at a profit to state procurement agencies.
Increased retail prices will eliminate the profits
of such transactions.

To offset the effect of increased prices in
urban living standards, wage earners and those who
receive state pensions will receive special monthly
supplemental payments of five yuan -- or an average
of about 10 percent of their income. According to
the calculations of the state, the value of the
subsidies provided will more than offset the increased outlays by consumers for nonstaple food
products. Most people, the government argues, will
be better off both because of the supplemental payments and because of November 1979 wage increases
for 40 percent of the labor force. Yet the price
increases have probably had negative incentive
effects on many workers. First, the average worker
over the past decades has become habituated to
price stability; price increases introduce a new
element of uncertainty in calculating the purchasing power of his wages. Second, the post-Mao
leadership had promised a system of regular wage
increases as a means of raising urban living standards -- not as a way of offsetting price inflation. Third, since the supplements are paid to
wage earners and pensioners only, families with a
high ratio of dependents to wage earners will
clearly have lower real incomes, even after the
wage supplements and the raises. Finally, millions
of workers employed in the collective sector will
not generally receive the full amount of the sub-
sidy and many will get nothing.

IMPLICATIONS FOR FOREIGN INVOLVEMENT

The readjustment of economic development policy has had far-reaching implications for China's

foreign economic policy. Only a year ago China seemed to be on the verge of acquiring an unprecedented volume of capital goods from abroad. But many of the tentative commitments that had been made with foreign firms focused on the steel sector. For example, Japanese and German consortia were negotiating a contract for construction of a $14 billion steel facility in North China with an annual capacity of ten million metric tons. U.S. Steel Corporation signed a protocol for the development of related iron ore mining and processing facilities, with an ultimate contract value of more than one billion dollars. But following a series of high level meetings in late 1978 and early 1979, the Chinese leadership sharply downgraded steel's priority and the negotiations for these mammoth facilities were broken off.

The cutbacks in foreign economic activity were not limited to the steel sector; they reflected the general reduction of investment and a renewed emphasis on conservative borrowing practices. Thus, Chinese leaders rejected other projects, such as proposals by Hyatt International and Intercontinental Hotels for luxury international class hotels, largely because of their high foreign exchange costs. They also questioned the wisdom of drawing on international credit lines -- almost $30 billion in credit had been extended by the international banking community by mid-1979 -- to accelerate the import of foreign plants and equipment. Chinese concern about how such a large volume of debt could be repaid was hardly irrelevant in view of the sharp limitations that were being placed by Western countries on the imports of China's major export item -- textiles. (In January 1979 the US had opened negotiations for "voluntary restriction" in Chinese textile exports. When it became clear that the Chinese were not sufficiently compliant, the US imposed quotas on the flow of Chinese textiles into the US market.) Consequently the Chinese minister of finance disclosed in June 1979 that China would draw on only a very small portion of the credits that had been extended. Instead, the Chinese adopted other innovative practices, discussed below, to accelerate their foreign trade.

By the end of 1979 the foreign economic strategy of the readjustment period had evolved to include several elements. First, there was vastly tightened central bureaucratic control of capital goods imports. For example, the Bank of China reasserted its crucial role in the approval of contracts. More importantly, Chinese planners began to explore seriously the means of acquiring advance management and production technology without buying capital goods. This prompted a fundamental reappraisal of China's approach of importing turnkey plants and of many such projects under negotiation.

Second, it was decided to accelerate trade and the acquisition of foreign technology via means that required less foreign exchange and, particularly, little external debt. Instead of drawing on foreign bank credit, even though offered at interest rates subsidized by national export-import banks, the Chinese have sought to make use of direct government-to-government loans. The latter typically have considerably longer repayment terms and even lower interest rates. The Japanese were first to offer such development aid, committing themselves initially to a $1.5 billion loan at 3 percent interest, to be repaid over thirty years beginning in the 1990s. These long-term low-interest government credits will be used to undertake major infrastucture projects such as port, railroad, and hydroelectric facilities that are essential for future economic growth.

To attract foreign technology while minimizing their own foreign exchange outlays, the Chinese are also welcoming direct foreign investment and encouraging the use of compensation trade. A joint venture law was promulgated in June 1979 to provide the broad legal framework for direct foreign investment in China. More detailed tax, corporation, and other codes, expected sometime in 1980, will pave the way for the completion of a number of joint venture agreements. Many of these, in agriculture, aquatic farming, light industry, machinery, electronics, tourism, and textiles, have been under negotiation for months. A large number of agreements for compensation trade have already been concluded. These include contracts for processing and assembling foreign goods in China as well as agreements under which the Chinese pay for foreign capital equipment imports by exporting the subsequent product.

Finally, the Chinese are trying to accelerate the growth of their own commodity exports and other forms of foreign exchange earnings in order to pay for a large share of imports on a current basis. One mechanism for accelerating exports is an expanded system of sharing foreign exchange earnings with local governments, thus encouraging them to emphasize, in the enterprises under their control,

production for foreign markets. The success of
these efforts is reflected in preliminary trade
statistics for 1979. Total commodity trade rose by
more than a third to 28 billion dollars. Exports
rose almost as much as imports, leaving a relatively small imbalance in merchandise trade to be
filled by foreign remittances, earnings on processing contracts, transportation and tourism, and
borrowing.

OUTLOOK

China begins the decade of the 1980s with a
short-run development strategy that is profoundly
different from that adopted only two years ago. In
many ways the new strategy is more balanced, recog-
nizing the need to redress shortcomings that have
emerged, and represents a somewhat more realistic
blueprint for future development. The shifts have
been accompanied by a reduction, at least in the
short run, in the potential role of foreign firms
in China's modernization and a concommitant rise in
the importance of increased efficiency in the use
of domestic resources.

Yet the outlook remains highly uncertain.
This uncertainty arises not simply because of problems of unemployment, inflation, and inadequate
housing, but rather because of continuing fundamental disagreement at the highest levels concerning the formulation and implementation of policy.
It is difficult to judge the severity of these policy disputes. But it should be recognized that
many of the imbalances that the new program ad-
dresses have actually existed for a decade or more.
Thus the readjustment program appears to represent
a significant change in the dominant policy objectives in Beijing, rather than simply a consensus
response to a new set of economic problems. The
new policy clearly reflects the reemergence of the
veteran economic planner Chen Yun, who in 1957 was
instrumental in designing an economic policy ad-
justment that is similar to that emerging in China
today. Chen, who had lost effective power during
the late 1950s and did not regain influence in the
1960s, made a dramatic comeback in late 1978 when
he became a member of the Politburo's standing committee.

The current debate focuses not only on the
economic plan for the remaining years of the readjustment phase and the subsequent Sixth Five Year
Plan, but even on the implementation of the 1979

Chen Yun (Eastfoto)

plan that was approved in June of that year. During 1979, many parts of the bureaucracy resisted implementing the cutbacks in investment that are at the heart of the readjustment program. Most obviously, the heavy industrial sector continued to press forward with a broad array of capital projects. By year's end, Beijing was engaged in an almost frantic program to insure that the planned reduction in investment projects was actually carried out and to try to step up the flow of resources to light industry, agriculture, energy, communications, and transportation. Until the final quarter of 1979 production of manufactured consumer goods was falling short of the plan because the priority allocation of electric power, fuel and other inputs had not been fully carried out.

Ironically the rapid recovery of agricultural production in 1978 and 1979 heightened the dispute over developmental priorities. The surge in output was perhaps gratifying to those who had argued for a restructuring of rural incentives and a massive flow of resources into agriculture. But those who have been critical of the basic thrust of the readjustment program are now arguing that the program's initial success justifies a return to the status quo ante -- a higher rate of investment and emphasis on the heavy industrial sector rather than agriculture and consumer goods. At the end of 1979 this debate was not confined to the academic and research institute periphery but was said to prevail among "leading cadres" and to make unified action impossible. Indeed, implementation of the previously endorsed policy was characterized as being a "hard battle."

The outlook is also clouded by an abrupt increase (20 percent) in military expenditures in 1979. Much of the 3.4 billion yuan increase may have been due to China's early 1979 military action against Vietnam. But the results of the confrontation may have led to a reassessment of China's military capabilities and a decision to maintain the military share of budgetary expenditure at its new higher level. This, of course, would reduce the ability of the regime to raise consumption expenditures without further reducing the share of investment.

The continued debate is far from an arcane exchange of alternative views. The apparent inability of the center to follow through fully on the new development policies threatens to exacerbate all of China's short-term problems. For example, if it is not possible to continue to reduce the rate of investment as planned for 1980 and to channel more resources into production of consumer goods, there will probably be inflationary pressure in retail markets, because the growth of purchasing power, particularly in the rural sector, will not be matched by an increased flow of consumer goods. Inflation, whether repressed or open, will set back efforts to raise labor productivity. The unscheduled continued flow of rsources to heavy industry aggravates the unemployment problem, for that sector has a far higher capital-labor ratio than light manufacturing. Thus a given amount of investment creates far fewer jobs when it is allocated to heavy industry rather than light industry. The longer run threat, of course, is that the debate over priorities will impair the ability of the center to formulate consistent plans for the remainder of the readjustment period and to agree on a longer run strategy for the Sixth Five Year Plan.

5
Painting with a New Brush: Art in Post-Mao China

Michael Sullivan

Protest art in Beijing. Paintings of nudes. The emergence of "art for art's sake." These are among the reports coming out of China since the "gang of four" fell from power in October 1976.

Such developments are being interpreted as a significant shift in the government's attitude toward art, and on a larger scale, as a liberalization of culture. Perhaps the most dramatic sign of the new tolerance was provided by the minister of culture himself. When asked if art must still serve the workers and peasants, Huang Zhen replied, "I think you can produce anything."

All this suggests that the rigid cultural policies formed under Mao have been relaxed, if not repudiated. Is this in fact the case? If so, is the new liberal climate for the arts likely to endure, or will it be followed by another swing of the pendulum back to tighter political control?

There is no simple answer to these questions because many factors are involved. Among them are the traditional Chinese willingness to accept authority and orthodoxy in cultural matters; the fact that the arts are practiced at many levels, from official cooperative projects such as the decoration of a public building to the private act of painting an album-leaf for a friend; and the need to distinguish between what is officially said and what is actually done.

Since 1949, art in China has both flourished and suffered. It has flourished in the sense that artists are respected and secure in their livelihood, and that the social base of artistic activity has broadened immeasurably: any peasant can be an amateur artist today. It has suffered to the degree that Party control has been successful. During the worst years, artists underwent severe persecution. Today, the climate is comparatively liberal, but there is no way of predicting the future.

To understand the lingering uncertainty in the minds of artists today we need only glance over the history of art in China since 1949. The first seven years were the honeymoon period. For the most part, artists supported the new regime and morale was high. But after the sudden wilting of the "hundred flowers" movement in 1957, when many found themselves labeled "poisonous weeds," a sense of insecurity was bred that still persists. The chaos of the Great Leap Forward (1958-1959) was followed by a campaign against "bourgeois rightist" elements (1963-1965), with emphasis on the art of the People's Liberation Army (PLA) and of peasants and workers. A widely publicized example was the elevation of the peasant art of the Huxian Production Brigade in Shaanxi province as a model for the masses. There is now a museum of peasant paintings at Huxian. What began as a spontaneous movement rooted in a local tradition ended up, for a few years at least, as a quasi-official style.

During these years (roughly 1950-1966), painters were encouraged to develop native styles and techniques, to paint in the traditional medium tractor drivers and oil refineries instead of long-robed scholars gazing at waterfalls. A certain amount of "Western" realism was introduced, especially in the painting of figures, but this stopped short of the use of shadows -- something the Chinese artist always prefers to avoid. These developments were not new. They had begun in the 1920s and 1930s under the influence of Western-trained artists such as Xu Beihong (1895-1953); but now, in the spirit of Mao's slogans "Make the past serve the present" and "Make foreign things serve China," they were given a new ideological urgency.

The guidelines for art after 1949 were those uncompromisingly socialist principles set down by Mao Zedong in his "Yanan Talks on Art and Literature" (1942). While acknowledging the value of China's artistic heritage, he stressed the overriding importance of political criteria. Artists and historians fell into line. To embrace the great art of the past produced for the "slave-owning" and "feudal" ruling class, it was held that the sacrificial bronzes of the Shang Dynasty, and Buddhist sculpture, bore witness to the skill of the laboring masses. The suggestive, elitist

painting of the scholar-gentry, which for centuries
constituted the "mainstream" in Chinese art, presented a problem. The problem was overcome by
stating that while the social attitudes of the artists were bad, they were a product of their time,
and their art was good -- indeed, that it was "realistic" in the sense that it contained the "es-
sence" of the birds and flowers, bamboo and landscape that they portrayed. What was attacked was
not the art but the social system in which it was
created. Realism as normally understood was to be
confined to pictures exposing the evils of pre-
Liberation society. Life in the People's Republic
of China had to be idealized, a kind of art that
came to be called "revolutionary romanticism."

All Chinese painting is to some extent symbol-
ic. A landscape, for example, is a visible mani-
festation of the cosmic Tao. The bamboo is a
symbol of the pliant but unbreakable spirit of the
scholar-official. In the PRC the red sun became a
symbol of Mao Zedong, the plum blossom in the snow
a symbol of the early Communist martyrs. Today, as
always in China, art must mean something. Form
alone, or emphasis on form over content ("bourgeois

Bai Xueshi, "The Red Flag Canal" (1973). An unusually monumental example of the modernized traditional technique to depict a contemporary subject.

formalism"), is not enough. This is the main reason why Western abstraction and abstract expressionism are of little interest to the Chinese.

How free is the Chinese artist? This is not a
new question. In the past the vast majority of
painters, even the most gifted, were content to
work within a recognized tradition even while they
advanced it. The out-and-out individualist in
China was always the exception and not the rule.
So the constraints on personal expression in post-
1949 China, while extremely severe at times, were
on the whole less intolerable to most artists than
would have been the case in the West.

The Cultural Revolution's first phase lasted
from 1966 to 1969, but the campaign against any
form of art not approved by the extremists dominated by Jiang Qing (Mao's wife and one of the
"gang of four") continued with increasing intensity
up to their downfall in October 1976. As early as
mid-1966 Jiang Qing had been given the power to
arrest her personal enemies. During these turbu-
lent years the artists' associations were disbanded
and art schools closed. Painters were dismissed,
jailed, or intimidated for alleged subversion. Li
Kuchan, for example, was vilified for painting in
monochrome ink eight lotus flowers for the International Club in Beijing -- their lack of positive,
cheerful color was taken by Jiang Qing as an attack
on the eight operas and ballets she had promoted.
Zhou Yang, head of the National Federation of Writers and Artists, hitherto regarded as a loyal supporter of Mao, was paraded through the streets like
a common criminal with a placard round his neck.
In 1972, Jiang Qing organized an exhibition of
"black art" along the lines of the Nazi's exhibitions of "Entartete Kunst" (degenerate art). The
parallel is not fortuitous. After the fall of the
"gang," cartoonists portrayed them as Nazis, with
Yao Wenyuan, the propaganda chief, as a reincarna-
tion of Joseph Goebbels.

Many artists looked to Premier Zhou Enlai for
protection, and must have been dismayed when he
appeared to let them suffer; but he protected some
of them discreetly, and secured them commissions
for paintings in public buildings. By 1975 he was
very ill, and on January 8, 1976 he died. Artists
felt their last refuge was gone, and now the control of the "gang" was complete. What this meant
to them is expressed in these lines from a poem
written later by the painter Huang Yongyu:

Huang Yongyu, "Red Lotus." Painted in mourning for
Zhou Enlai on the night after he died, January 8/9,
1976.

People cursed in the street
Shedding silent tears,
Sighing alone at night,
Hearing their neighbors
Weeping quietly.

Every trainload was full of calamity;
Every home was filled with foreboding.
Even the most law-abiding citizens swore in
anger,
While those who sang well lost their voices.

When people heard the truth, they had to keep
it secret,
While blatant lies printed in the newspapers
were holy gospel.
All people old and young became good actors,
While all professional actors' faces were
expressionless.

There was such a time. . . .

On April 4/5, 1976 an immense gathering on
Tiananmen Square to mourn Zhou Enlai was harshly
put down. Cultural oppression continued unabated
until the fall of the "gang of four" six months
later, when the news of the arrest of Jiang Qing
was greeted with joy. At once the clouds began to
lift, and cultural life started to recover. The
art schools were reopened, artists returned to
their old jobs, and in 1978 the National Federation
of Writers and Artists was reestablished. Old arts
were revived and their ideological content began to
soften. For example, the New Year pictures produced at Yangliujing in Shandong province once
again depict, instead of workers and their trac-
tors, fat naked babies in pinafores and other traditional symbols of prosperity.
An urgent task was to reeducate people about
the arts. The art journals had ceased publication
in 1966, and before that their content had been
heavily political. Now Meishu (Art) and Meishu-
yanjiu (Art Research) reappeared. The political
message is still there in the attacks on modern
"formalist" movements in Western art such as abstract expressionism. But traditional Western art
is carefully studied and the nude, forbidden by
Jiang Qing as bourgeois decadence, is studied in
the art schools. As a work-study student in Paris
in 1921, Zhou Enlai had collected postcards of
works of art, including nudes by Rodin and Girodet;

now these are reproduced with his comments in Mei-shu, while Jiang Qing's attack on the nude is lik-ened in the same journal to the reactionary Pope Sixtus V causing the nude figures in Michelangelo's "Last Judgement" to be modestly draped. The study of the nude is now considered "scientific," and an aid to realism. Chinese appear to be puzzled by the amount of fuss this question has aroused abroad.

How much freer artists have become since the fall of the "gang" is hard to gauge. It is doubt-ful that Huang Zhen's "I think you can produce anything" should be taken too literally. In fact, a range of views exist. In a 1978 article entitled "A Hundred Flowers Bloom Again" one writer extols the renaissance that has undoubtedly taken place since 1976, but goes on to lay down six political criteria for art, including the following: it must help consolidate the people's dictatorship, it must help strengthen the leadership of the Communist Party, and it must be beneficial to socialist international unity. Provided it adheres to these principles, the writer adds, "then any subject can be adopted. . . . We encourage our writers and art-ists to evolve and further develop their individual styles through arduous practice and tireless exper-iment."

By contrast, a much more flexible line was taken by the rehabilitated Zhou Yang, speaking at the Fourth National Congress of Writers and Artists in Beijing (October 30 to November 16, 1979). He noted that circumstances had changed since Mao set out his directives for art: "We are confronted with new problems unknown to the writers of the Marxists classics, Mao included. . . ." Further-more, "We should integrate Marxist theory with the practice of the literary and art movement of China, with the long cultural tradition of our country." These two pronouncements conflict, so, as is often necessary, one should look at what is actually done as well as at what is officially said.

The signs of a more sophisticated attitude toward art could be seen in the big retrospective exhibition held in the Beijing National Gallery in the autumn of 1979, marking thirty years of the PRC. One large hall showed propaganda paintings in both the Chinese and Western media, another dis-played mixed subjects, and a third was devoted to pictures mourning Zhou Enlai. There was no room allocated exclusively to Mao. Many of the pictures in the Zhou hall showed the dramatic events of

April 1976 in Tiananmen Square, the intensity of grief, the passionate reciting of poems, the heroic young women defending the wreaths from the militia. No event in recent Chinese history has inspired so intense and so widely shared an outpouring of emotion in which public and private feelings were fused.

The Memorial Hall to Mao Zedong, built in 1977, is also an important indication of recent trends. Its architecture is monumental but undistinguished, a synthesis of many designs, said to be inspired by the Lincoln Memorial. But leading painters such as Li Keran and Guan Shanyue were commissioned to decorate the interior with big landscapes in the traditional style. The place of honor behind the seated marble statue of Mao was given to a huge landscape in tapestry designed by Huang Yongyu. A happier choice could not have been made, since Huang is one of the most creative artists to have emerged in the last twenty years. Significantly, this landscape contains no hint of propaganda, and Huang is a younger artist outside the art establishment, where age and seniority still count for much.

Artists today in the big cities are restless, hungry for new styles and foreign contacts which they are establishing partly through their counterparts in Hong Kong, and partly through an intense interest in the less avant-garde trends in contemporary Japanese art. In the 1960s the Fifth Moon Group in Taipei were pioneers in the new Chinese abstract expressionism. In the 1970s the focus shifted to the Circle Group and other groups in Hong Kong, who are now beginning to introduce new styles to the more advanced artists in the PRC. It is too soon to see whether this will eventually lead to Chinese art becoming part of the international movement in modern art, but this is not impossible if present trends continue. Such is China's cultural pride and self-respect, however, that these stimuli are unlikely to lead to that instant copying of foreign art that the Japanese achieved so skillfully. When asked why he worked in oils, a foreign technique, the painter Wu Guanzhong said that when a Chinese takes up the brush to paint in oils, it becomes Chinese painting.

This hunger for new ideas, stopping short of abstraction and other contemporary Western movements, has produced a great variety of styles. Artists are seeking inspiration in ancient art, notably in the Buddhist frescoes at Dunhuang, and

Ai Xuan, "Protecting the Wreathes" (1978). A dramatic memory of the Tiananmen Incident, April 4/5, 1976.

are delving into art books that survived the Cultural Revolution or have since been imported from abroad. For example, the ancient Chinese poems, Songs of the South, are illustrated by Pan Jieje in a decorative style inspired by Edmund Dulac -- which the artist could only have seen in reproduction. A painting by Ai Xuan of a young woman with arms outspread defending the wreaths at Tienanmen is inspired by the relief by Vauthier on the wall of the Père-Lachaise Cemetery in Paris commemorating the Communards executed there in 1871.

Not all these eclectic experiments are equally successful. The decorations in the Beijing International Airport (1979) range from stylized mythological scenes in the manner of the Dunhuang frescoes to figures in the Art Déco style of the 1930s, and scenes in which, perhaps for the first time in a Chinese public building, the nude figure appears, although these nudes have since been covered up. The fact that these airport decorations are chiefly for foreign eyes suggests a disturbing tendency to create a different cultural ambience for the foreigner, and to pander to the tourist trade. With

Yuan Yunsheng, "Water Festival -- Song of Life" (1979). Detail from a wall mural depicting China's Dai minority which appears in a dining room for foreign visitors, Beijing International Airport.

the old taste-creating classes of the court and the scholar-officials swept away, there is little guidance or certainty in matters of taste. At the same time, the growing sophistication of the city dweller is widening once more the enormous gap between the educated and the peasants that Mao tried so hard to close.

Such a gap is already leading toward the establishment of a new cultural elite -- perhaps essential for the highest achievement, but disastrous for the advance of revolutionary ideals. There is always the danger of a backlash against elitist culture on the part of less privileged urban workers, although the peasants, already far behind, are unlikely to know enough to care very much. This danger, and the ever-present fear that the Party line may shift again, must make all but the boldest artists extremely cautious. The curtailing of freedom of speech in the spring of 1980 is likely to be followed by less freedom for art, and in the present climate it seems improbable that exhibitions of dissident art, like that held in Beijing in late 1979, will often be tolerated.

Instances of such anti-establishment cultural activity in China are rare, and their importance is apt to be exaggerated in the foreign press. Nevertheless, although a return to the intoxicating sense of freedom that followed the fall of the "gang of four" is unlikely, the climate for the arts appears to be healthier today than at any time since the establishment of the People's Republic of China.

6
Recent Chinese Literature: A Second Hundred Flowers

Leo Ou-fan Lee

Even the most diligent observer in the West has difficulty keeping up with the tremendous pace of change that is taking place in all aspects of Chinese life. The field of literature is certainly no exception. Since the fall of the "gang of four" in October 1976, a process of gradual liberalization has been underway. As of this writing, it promises to be of greater scope and consequence than the previous period of literary thaw -- the first "hundred flowers" of 1956-1957.

During the past two or three years, some 3,000 literary journals have appeared throughout China. Old writers and old works have reemerged; former "rightists" and victims of the Cultural Revolution are writing again. Masterpieces of Chinese and Western literature, both traditional and modern, are being reissued.

Societies have been formed for the study of Dream of the Red Chamber (the most esteemed of all traditional Chinese novels) and Lu Xun (the foremost modern Chinese writer). A few short stories from Taiwan have been reprinted, sometimes without the permission of the authors. In September 1979, two PRC authors attended a "Chinese Weekend" at the University of Iowa where for the first time they met with writers and scholars from Taiwan, Hong Kong, and the United States. Earlier in the year, two eminent writers from China -- the novelist Ba Jin and the poet Ai Qing -- toured Europe and met with enthusiastic receptions. The well-known dramatist Cao Yu toured the United States in April 1980.

Sizable numbers of translations from Western literature are being published or are planned for publication. Some of the new literary journals have featured short stories by such contemporary American writers as Isaac Singer, Saul Bellow, John Updike, and John Cheever. A conference on American literature was held recently at Shandong University, and two anthologies of American short stories are being published. At least four societies for the study of foreign literature have been organized, and one journal contains a learned treatise on French structuralism. Western plays in Chinese translation (Brecht's Galileo, Arthur Miller's All My Sons) have been performed to packed houses, as have guest performances of Hamlet by the Old Vic from England (with simultaneous translation by a complete Chinese cast) and concerts by the Boston Symphony Orchestra. A new wave of Westernism seems about to inundate the urban population of China.

Perhaps the most significant event since 1976 has been the convening of the Fourth National Congress of Writers and Artists in Beijing in late 1979. Some 3,200 representatives gathered in the Great Hall of the People to hear speeches by political and literary leaders, and to discuss future directions in art and literature. Vice Premier Deng Xiaoping provided the keynote: art and literature must follow their own "special characteristics" and "principles of development." The promotion of artistic standards must have priority over Party control in order to realize a second "blooming" of the "hundred flowers." The general consensus which emerged was summarized in a concluding speech by the veteran dramatist Xia Yan who said, "In art and literature there must be an emancipation of thought."

Yet behind these hopeful signs of a more active and independent Chinese literature, there also seems to be a pervasive sense of uncertainty. Following the official anti-"gang of four" campaign, writers united in condemning the Cultural Revolution (1966-1976) as a decade of unprecedented nightmare. The more conscientious among them have also embarked on a process of soul-searching, of trying to find out what exactly went wrong in Chinese society during the Cultural Revolution. The result has been as shockingly tragic as the current activism is hopeful.

Just two years ago, a collection of short stories, The Execution of Mayor Yin and Other Stories from the Great Proletarian Cultural Revolution (Indiana University Press, 1978), by an émigré Chinese writer, Chen Jo-hsi, was published in the United States. It generated considerable attention as the

first example of "dissident literature" from the
People's Republic. Whether dissident or not, the
book unveiled to Western readers a radically different picture of life from that portrayed by effu-
sive Western travelers or by official Chinese publications such as People's Daily and China Recon-
structs. Chen's stories presented a gallery of
ordinary people, mostly in the cities, who were
caught in the maelstrom of the Cultural Revolution.
Based on her own experience during a seven-year
stay in China (1966-1973), these stories bring out
the poignancy and irony of human suffering for a
"revolutionary" cause which eluded comprehension by
most Chinese people because of its constantly
changing nature and confusing campaigns and slogans. It was a dark, yet intensely human vision
which Chen provided the reader, a view at odds with
some reports of the PRC as a socialist, egalitarian
utopia.

Today, the book's contents seem dated. Reve-
lations from China's official press confront us
with an even darker picture of the excesses attri-
buted to the "gang of four" during the past decade.
In the name of discrediting the "gang" and its followers, writers inside China have been emboldened
to reveal their past "wounds." Several works appeared in 1977-1978. Their theme is reflected in a
now famous story, "Shanghen" ("Scars" or "Wounds");
thus they have become known as "literature of the
wounded" (shanghen wenxue). Most of these works
are artistically inferior to Chen Jo-hsi's stories.
But in their very crudity of style and technique
they disclose an unadorned truth: contemporary
Chinese society under socialism is, in fact,
fraught with problems.

Although the "gang of four" is conveniently
used as a scapegoat, some of the problems call into
question the raison d'être of the Cultural Revolution itself. For instance, in the story "Principal
Teacher" by Liu Xinwu, the most celebrated writer
of this "wounded generation," the central issue
concerns a teenage "true believer" whose very self-
righteousness about her political convictions --
blind parroting of empty political slogans -- becomes the source of her psychological problems. In
another story by Liu, "The Place of Love," a dedicated young couple are guilt-ridden about their mutual sentiments of love which they consider incom-
patible with their revolutionary duties. In both
stories, it takes a patient old cadre to help the
youngsters see the errors of their blind ideologi-

cal ways.

While most of these stories adhere to a certain imperative of faith in the system, particularly in giving positive roles to veteran cadres who were besmeared by the "gang of four," subsequent works have not been constrained by any political positivism. It seems that the ethos of exposé has opened a Pandora's box, and each is more daring and bitter than the previous work, ultimately implying a larger evil rooted in the socio-political system itself.

A most recent cause scandale is a lengthy exposé written by an erstwhile "rightist" author, Liu Binyan. He describes in plodding documentary fashion a true case of corruption of monumental proportions. The piece was published in the official journal People's Literature, in September 1979, and created an instant "earthquake." Its sensational contents are matched by an equally sensational title, "Between Men and Monsters," with the obvious implication that such monstrosities of human behavior cannot be explained away by accusing a limited number of individuals; the cause of corruption must be traced to the entire bureaucracy and even to the socialist system.

Liu Binyan is reported as saying that he no longer cares if he is again purged as a rightist, since he has already suffered twenty years of silence. For Liu, Wang Meng, and other writers who have surfaced again after a long period of disgrace, the present thaw represents more than another "hundred flowers." For them, writing is now an existential justification and personal vindication. Otherwise their twenty-year silence would hold no meaning.

Older writers who survived the Cultural Revolution with varying degrees of personal "wounds" are in a more tragic position: some, like Ba Jin, have mustered enough courage to write again; others can only bemoan the passing of their less fortunate colleagues. The current literary press is filled with articles of condolence and reminiscence which voice not merely unquenchable sorrow but perhaps even irrepressible guilt. The most moving piece of personal reminiscence is Ba Jin's "Remembering Xiao Shan." It is a gentle, yet powerful, essay in memory of his beloved wife who died during the Cultural Revolution, a literary equivalent of "J'accuse."

It is reported that Yang Hansheng, another veteran writer, read aloud at the Fourth Congress a list of more than a hundred names -- all writers

and artists who died during the Cultural Revolution. This commemorative gesture elicited a
searching question from Liu Xinwu, on behalf of his
senior colleagues: while the revolutionary martyrs
of the 1930s had died for a worthy cause, why was
it that writers and artists who have dedicated
their lives to the country and the people in socialist society since 1949 still have to die? Liu
further stated that as he witnessed the living veterans -- victims of political disgrace like Xia
Yan, Liu Binyan, and Wang Meng -- he was strengthened in his conviction that there should be no more
anti-rightist campaigns: "We must be on our guard
against the extreme left and fight against the extreme left!"

* * *

The current phenomenon of social criticism and
soul-searching also has a historical dimension.
The watershed dates for modern Chinese literature
are May Fourth (1919) and April Fifth (1976). May
Fourth marked the high point of the New Culture
Movement, modern China's intellectual revolution;
April Fifth was the date of the unprecedented Tiananmen Square demonstrations, seen as the beginning
of a new popular consciousness following the Communist Revolution of 1949.*
In this coupling of dates (which in Chinese
language conveys a neat numerical pun: wusi [5/4]
and siwu [4/5]), the reigning slogans of the May
Fourth Movement -- freedom, democracy, and science
-- are associated with the new slogan of "four modernizations." From a literary perspective, however, the May Fourth spirit -- the legacy of New Literature since the literary revolution of 1917 --
stands esentially for the role of the writer as
critic, as a voice of social conscience.
The undisputed model, the writer who embodied

---

*The Tiananmen Square demonstrations commemor-
ated the death of Zhou Enlai. This unusual exhibit
of vox populi was marked by hundreds, if not thousands, of poems written for the occasion. Several
collections of Tiananmen poetry have been published; one collection is graced by Chairman Hua
Guofeng's calligraphy on the cover. An English
translation of some thirty poems is now available
under the title The Tiananmen Poems, edited and
translated by Xiao Lan (Beijing: Foreign Languages
Press, 1979).

the very best of this critical tradition, is Lu Xun (1861-1936). Although Lu Xun was posthumously deified, especially by Mao Zedong himself, his disciples -- those writers who have inherited his "true grit" and his fearless integrity -- have been the victims of successive political campaigns since the 1940s. Thus, those who now remember Lu Xun's spirit in a larger historical context also recall the fate of his disciples: Hu Feng, Xiao Jun, and Feng Xuefeng were the most prominent to be purged. (In the case of Hu Feng, the order reportedly came from Mao himself.)

An important legacy of Lu Xun and of the literature of the 1930s has been what might be called critical realism -- the realistic exposure of social ills in order to hasten reform. Lu Xun's writing, particularly his voluminous essays, epitomized this spirit of fearless criticism despite censorship and opposition by the Chinese Nationalist Party. Since the Communist Party in the 1930s was not strong enough to dictate literary policy, the leftist writers felt compelled to form a self-styled vanguard against the "White Terror" under the Nationalists. Thus, despite controls imposed by the League of Left-Wing Writers, they were in

Lu Xun (1861-1936), social critic and author, is often called the "father of modern Chinese literature." Woodcut by Zhao Ruizhun and Wu Yongliang, "Lu Xun with Young Writers and Artists."

fact allowed considerable independence and enough
flexibility to evolve their own independent visions
of society.

The legacy of May Fourth was eventually repudiated by no less a figure than Mao Zedong. In his
famous "Yanan Talks on Art and Literature" in 1942,
Mao declared that the new imperative was to extol
the virtues of the people. Critical realism should
be replaced by socialist realism, and literature
and art must be more populist in orientation. The
writer's individual vision of society should be
subordinated to a collective vision. Buoyed by a
prevailing temper of patriotism, optimism, and ide-
alism, leftist writers in the Yanan era up through
the early 1950s were eager to respond to Mao's
clarion call to "learn from the people" and to
write authentically about the lives of peasants,
workers, and soldiers.

But in following Maoist guidelines, writers in
the early 1950s still retained a degree of artistic
independence, not necessarily in opposition to any
official policies, but in the sense of having the
right to develop one's own interpretation of the
new society. Then, starting in the mid-1950s, a
crescendo of campaigns was launched to purge writers of their residual individualism and to trans-
form them into genuine proletarians in both thought
and behavior. The Cultural Revolution can be
viewed as a culmination in this process of radical
transformation.

It is now generally agreed that the Cultural
Revolution went too far. Its destructive mania put
an end to an era of precarious "liberalism" and the
creativity of the 1950s, during which some significant works had appeared: Ding Ling's The Sun
Shines Over the Songgan River, Zhou Libo's Hurri-
cane, Liang Bin's Red Flags, and Yang Mo's The Song
of Youth, to name a few. Under the policies of
Jiang Qing (Mao's wife), the Maoist imperative to
extol reached unprecedented heights: only the
bright side of life and struggle, portrayed in the
most heroic light, was allowed. The result was a
corpus of "popular" literature and art which became
uninspiring even to the less educated people for
whom it was ostensibly created. Jiang Qing's "model operas" were a particular disappointment. Only
a few works of art and literature -- such as Hao
Ran's novels and the peasant paintings of Huxian
(nurtured since the late 1950s) -- managed to capture a sense of revolutionary ebullience. But
these were exceptions to what many observers have

since called a "cultural desert."

Given the dismal record in art and literature during the Cultural Revoution, a swing of the pendulum toward the other pole was perhaps inevitable. Shortly after the fall of the "gang of four" in 1976, some of the wall posters and semi-underground publications (often in mimeographed form) began to call for an end to political and ideological interference in art and literature. An "open letter" to the editor of Wenyi Bao (Literary Gazette), which first appeared on Beijing's Democracy Wall on January 21, 1979, demanded that political censorship of writers be abolished altogether: "In history, an individual might commit this or that error or have this or that problem. But if his writings are of good quality, why should the writings be condemned because of the author's problems?" The letter further stated that "no standards should be allowed to exist and to be measured by a few people"; literary works should be read and judged by the masses of readers themselves, their value tested by time.

The underground initiative has surfaced to become the basis of an unofficial movement to reassert the dignity and worth of literature -- an indirect rebuttal to the main thrust of Mao's "Yanan Talks." According to a recent report, slogans such as "literature is literature" and "art is art" are widespread. This plea for de-politicization has also given renewed attention to the study of literary theory: Marxist as well as traditional Chinese theories of literature are again being read and discussed. The obvious implication is that the Maoist canon is one guideline, but not the only one.

There has been a related effort to broaden the subject matter treated in literature: love, romance, adventure, and even sex (apparently the themes of several underground novels during the Cultural Revolution) are now championed as permissible. At several forums on creative writing, new writers have been calling for the "promotion of artistic standards"; some have specifically raised the issue of subtle characterization, the importance of poetic imagery, and the need for a personal style. If these trends continue, the introduction of Taiwan literature could eventually have a profound impact on creative writing on the mainland, since recent Taiwan fiction is technically superior, though also dealing with realistic urban and rural themes.

Counterreactions to the rapid swing toward the

so-called "right" are already apparent. A great debate is now underway in the major literary journals: should writers continue to expose past wrongs or should they forget about the past and extol the future? Should they continue to break into more "proscribed areas" of the Maoist orthodoxy or should they treat literature as an "instrument" of class struggle? Have they gone too far in portraying the flaws of present society or have they not penetrated deeply enough? As of this writing, it seems that the proponents of liberalization still hold sway over tacit sympathizers of the radical line.

The situation in Chinese literature has indeed reached a critical stage. How long will the thaw last? Will there be a "leftist" backlash which might lead to a return of the radical revolutionary policies? A recent "science fiction" story which first appeared on the Democracy Wall (which has since been closed down) warns gloomily of a totalitarian China in the year 2001 ruled by a new power elite, following the death of the present leader. Yet there are still optimists who consider that present-day China has already reached a point of no return -- whatever new obstacles may arise in the future, they argue, the radical nightmare is gone forever. Only time can give the final answer to a question posed by a Red Guard manifesto which seems to capture the concerns of many Chinese: whither China?

Even if the present thaw should prove short-lived, the dynamism of the past few years is sufficient to render this second "blooming" a most impressive, if not tragic chapter in the history of modern Chinese literature.

7
Chinese Foreign Policy in 1979

Robert A. Scalapino

In the aftermath of the Soviet intervention in Afghanistan, Chinese leaders have some reason to be grimly satisfied with their earlier predictions. As the decade of the 1980s dawns, the persistent Chinese warnings that the world is headed for greater turmoil and that Soviet hegemonic goals represent a global menace, if not irrevocably proven, have greater plausibility. At the same time, the Chinese response to the Soviet action, apart from a torrent of verbal criticism, has been cautious, mirroring China's reluctance to risk conflict with a nation whose policies Beijing detests, but whose power it respects.

THE KEY PRINCIPLES

In surveying Chinese foreign policy, it is necessary to make a distinction between tactics and strategy. Beijing's recent tactics have ranged from war in Vietnam to negotiations in Moscow, and represent attempts to fulfill what PRC leaders perceive as China's national interest. Yet the strategy pursued has remained essentially unchanged: to compensate for China's multiple weaknesses by encouraging the broadest possible united front against the growing power and expansionist tendencies of the USSR.

The PRC retains three instruments through which its foreign policies can be effected, namely, relations between states, peoples, and comrades. Increasingly, however, ties to Communist parties have been weakened while intergovernmental relations have grown stronger.

Chinese leaders pay lip service to the links with "fraternal socialist nations," but the ideo-

75

logical component in Chinese foreign policy is now
strictly subordinated to a pragmatic balance of
power approach, in line with the major traditions
of Chinese culture. The leaders in Beijing ask few
ideologically oriented questions in competing for
Third World support, or in seeking to expand Chinese ties with the advanced industrial world, including the United States.

Homage is still paid to the Maoist concept of
a world divided into three parts: "the superpowers," a Second World composed of the capitalist
states of West Europe and Japan, and a heterogen-
eous Third World of developing states, with which
the PRC seeks to identify itself. But Chinese
spokesmen currently argue that only the broadest
possible cooperation among "advanced" and "developing" states can serve to deter Soviet aggression,
and specific Chinese policies have been fashioned
to this end.

INDOCHINA

In terms of basic PRC objectives, Indochina
represented China's greatest setback in 1979. The
brief Sino-Vietnamese war that opened in February
settled nothing. If China's aim was to force a
Vietnamese withdrawal from Cambodia and so provide
time for the Pol Pot forces to regroup and gain
strength, the effort failed. Moreover, the military thrust revealed serious weaknesses of both
weaponry and command in the People's Liberation
Army. Nor was the political cost negligible. Old
concerns regarding the threat of Chinese overlord-
ship were rekindled in Southeast Asia, and dismay
was registered in Japan and the United States.

On the other hand, the northernmost portion of
Vietnam was subjected to heavy punishment. More
importantly, China has signalled clearly that its
future passiveness in the face of a Vietnamese
quest for empire cannot be assumed, thus necessi-
tating the emplacement of large Vietnamese forces
along the China border.

Developments in Indochina should have been
predictable. Once the Vietnamese Communists won
the war against US and South Vietnamese forces,
their drive for hegemony over Cambodia and Laos was
inevitable. Only the timing and the means were in
doubt. Equally predictable was Chinese opposition
to a Vietnamese empire on its southern border.
That opposition would have manifested itself even
if Hanoi had not formed an alignment with the So-

viet Union. The Moscow-Hanoi alliance only made Beijing's resistance the more intense. The Chinese see developments here as a part of Russia's global strategy, that of using surrogates to expand Soviet power and encircle China.

China's leaders intend to keep their options open with respect to Indochina. Military pressure via border troop concentrations; assistance to all anti-Vietnamese Khmer guerillas and to dissidents in Laos, along with efforts to build a political coalition among such forces, and even to provoke splits in Hanoi's ruling circle; and the threat of renewed war -- all of these tactics have been signalled, and most are being employed. China has no intention of accepting the status quo in Indochina. It hopes to mix patience, toughness, and flexibility in a combination that will ultimately prove effective.

Present trends are not favorable for Beijing. The Vietnamese have been winning militarily. They too are tough and persevering. Soviet assistance has been substantial, reaching US $2.5 to $3 million a day. No effective Khmer coalition against the Heng Samrin-Hanoi regime is in sight, nor are political conditions in Laos presently hopeful. Yet, in a protracted, multi-faceted struggle, the Chinese believe that time is on their side. They have a cultural and geographic proximity denied the Russians, and a size that dwarfs that of Vietnam. Will not Russia's leaders tire at some point of the unending drain represented by their Indochina commitment? Will not the Vietnamese leaders exhaust their people in trying to control the Khmer and Laotian populations? Whether this be wishful thinking or a shrewd appraisal, it serves to justify present Chinese policies in the region.

RELATIONS WITH THE ASEAN STATES

Elsewhere in Southeast Asia, Chinese policies have paid great dividends. Helped by Hanoi's expansionist and refugee policies, Beijing has gained favor in its competition with the Soviet-Vietnamese bloc for the affections of ASEAN (Association of Southeast Asian Nations).

Thailand, for one, has interacted closely with the PRC out of concern over the growing Vietnamese threat. A complex situation has resulted. The Thai government is accused by Hanoi of providing a sanctuary for Pol Pot and other guerillas, and allowing the Chinese to use its territory as a supply

route for them. In response, the Beijing authorities publicly commit themselves to support Bangkok
in the event of a Vietnamese attack. The risks on
every side are high, and continuing conflict on its
borders has wreaked havoc with Thailand's domestic
tranquility.
      Not all of the ASEAN states are strongly dis-
posed toward the PRC, to be sure. Indonesia continues to harbor doubts about China's ultimate in-
tentions in Southeast Asia, doubts shared to some
extent by Malaysia and Singapore. Despite general
improvement in state-to-state relations, moreover,
and periodic assurances that "revolution cannot be
exported," the PRC seeks to retain links with most
guerrilla communist movements of the region, partly
as a means of influencing behavior on the part of
the governments concerned. This may prove more
difficult for Beijing, however, if it continues to
support the governments in power in the ASEAN
group. In any case, on balance, China has benefited from recent Vietnamese actions and the growing physical presence of the USSR in Indochina, a
combination of developments most unpalatable to the
ASEAN states. The Soviet intervention in Afghanistan has only heightened anxieties, with all five
of the ASEAN states condemning Soviet actions.
This event may have been one factor in Indonesia's
decision, announced in early 1980, to reestablish
diplomatic relations with the PRC.

KOREA

      In Northeast Asia, trends have also been
mixed. For the first time in many years, China
appears to be finding greater competition from the
Soviet Union in the contest for influence in North
Korea. Until recently, this contest was clearly
won by Beijing. Indeed, Soviet-North Korean relations have been cool to hostile for more than a
decade, despite Pyongyang's continued dependence
upon the Soviet Union for both military and economic assistance. Current developments are clouded,
but there are indications that Moscow has taken
certain initiatives in the last eighteen months to
improve matters. If this is the case, the results
thus far are not dramatic. North Korea together
with Romania refused to give a public endorsement
of the Afghanistan venture. Nonetheless, some suspect that Kim Il-song, the North Korean dictator,
is not entirely happy with recent Chinese policies.
      Moscow's answer to the growing Sino-American

entente may well be continued efforts to strengthen its buffer state system. A revised North Korea policy would be one example, the intrusion into Afghanistan another. Together with its support for Vietnamese dominance of Indochina, these represent a Soviet strategy to contain China pending any improvement in Sino-Soviet relations. The PRC response thus far has been its "soft" line toward North Korea, in sharp contrast with its "hard" line toward Vietnam, and the contest is far from concluded.

JAPAN

The Sino-Soviet contest for the affections of Japan continues to be lopsidedly favorable to Beijing. The Sino-Japanese peace and friendship treaty, signed in 1978, greatly angered the Russians. Chinese leaders continue to encourage Japanese nationalist demands for the return of the four northern islands, just off the coast of Hokkaido, occupied and now fortified by the Russians. They also champion Japan's rearmament "to defend itself against Soviet aggression." Japan, in turn, has made significant strides in its goal of fueling the Chinese industrial revolution. In 1979, bilateral trade reached some $7.5 billion, and at the end of the year, Prime Minister Ohira promised in Beijing an initial governmental loan of $1.5 billion.

Soviet policies, meanwhile, remain basically tough, as the Russians seek to confront Japan with the alternatives of improved economic relations or close-in, heightened, Soviet military power. In a recent poll, Japanese public opinion indicated that next to the United States, China was the nation with which the Japanese citizenry desired closer ties. And by a wide margin, the Soviet Union was voted the nation most disliked.

From Tokyo's view there are limits to the Sino-American-Japanese entente. Japan does not favor an anti-Soviet united front; it is not interested in being the spearhead of a high-risk, high-cost policy of confrontation with the USSR. Yet, Chinese relations with Japan today stand in sharp contrast with the continued deterioration of Soviet-Japanese relations.

SINO-SOVIET RELATIONS

China's energies in the foreign policy arena fall quite naturally into two categories: activities in East Asia, the area of China's vital interests and where its reach -- militarily, politically, and economically -- is the greatest; and relations with the "superpowers." In the second category, 1979 proved to be an eventful year.

In April, Beijing's leaders signified their wish to abrogate the Sino-Soviet Treaty of 1950, a treaty long honored in the breach. At the same time, they indicated a willingness to discuss means of improving state-to-state relations with the Russians, and after lengthy preliminaries, such talks got underway in the fall. So far, they have come to naught. The Soviets, true to their history in such matters, sought Chinese agreement to statements of general principles -- a pledge to eschew the use of either nuclear or conventional weapons by both parties, and guarantees not to seek hegemony. The Chinese insisted upon the resolution of specific issues first, including Soviet troop withdrawal from the People's Republic of Mongolia and a termination of military aid to Vietnam.

Despite the massive gap between Russian and Chinese positions, a new era in Sino-Soviet relations was forecast by some Soviet observers. They argued that, while initial progress would be minimal, both nations would eventually find it in their interest to reduce tension and begin the process of reconciliation. Some developments supported this contention: Sino-Soviet trade continued to grow, as did indications of debate with the PRC over the issue of relations with the USSR. Whatever the logic underwriting a limited Sino-Soviet detente, however, the immediate signs were strongly negative as 1979 came to a close, reinforced by the Soviet invasion of Afghanistan. After this event, the PRC government announced that negotiations would not be resumed in the spring of 1980 as had been agreed.

TIES WITH THE UNITED STATES

With the other "superpower," China's ties became ever closer. The strengthening of Sino-American relations throughout 1979 was first and foremost a testimony to (and in part, a cause of) the deteriorating relations between the USSR and the United States as well as the impasse in Sino-Soviet relations. In the economic arena, US-PRC trade reached $2 billion, scarcely the figure predicted earlier by enthusiasts, and far below Sino-Japanese trade, but well above the 1978 figure. Most obstacles to future economic intercourse, moreover, were removed. An agreement on claims and frozen assets was reached and, reversing a previous decision, the Carter administration asked Congressional approval of most-favored-nation treatment for China without simultaneously requesting similar treatment for the USSR. Legislative approval was granted in early 1980.

On the Chinese side, encouragement was given to foreign loans and capital investment. As 1979 ended, it appeared that the Chinese were about to enter their first joint ventures, at least one of them involving an American company. Certain problems or issues remained. Some laws pertaining to taxes, wages, and repatriation of profits had not yet been promulgated. Agreement on quotas for Chinese textiles and other commodities was not achieved, and Washington subsequently applied certain quotas unilaterally. Generally, Japan continued to hold its commanding lead in economic relations with the PRC. Prime Minister Ohira, in the course of his Beijing visit, re-emphasized Japan's avid interest in serving as the principal external contributor to China's industrial revolution. Nonetheless, economic relations between the US and the PRC looked promising to some observers, with trade of between $6-$8 billion being predicted for 1985.

Whether or not such predictions prove valid, China pursued its economic interests via scientific and technological exchanges with the United States. The Chinese students sent to the United States (as well as those going to Japan and other parts of the West) were overwhelmingly specializing in the physical sciences and technology. Almost 1,000 students, many of them at the post-doctoral level, arrived during 1979, and there are estimates that over 2,000 will be in the US by the end of 1980. US scientists, especially those of Chinese origin, were encouraged to lecture in China, and to establish intellectual ties with their counterparts. Even in the social sciences, Chinese leaders chose to give emphasis to management training (along with Soviet studies).

In the political-security realm, meanwhile, US-PRC relations also underwent significant development, symbolized by the visit of Secretary of Defense Harold Brown in early January 1980. When

Vice President Mondale visited China in August
1979, he called for the building of "concrete political ties in the context of mutual security," an
unprecedented signal to the world (especially the
Soviet Union) that America's united front advocates
were gaining ground. At the time of the Brown visit, President Carter reiterated privately that, for
the present, the United States would not sell military weapons to the PRC lest it jeopardize prospects for renewed US-Soviet detente. Later, however, the US and China agreed to take "parallel actions" to counter Soviet aggression in Afghanistan.
American sales of certain high technology products
and military-related equipment such as trucks, communications gear, and early warning radar were also
approved, as were exchanges of military delega-
tions. The United States had previously stated
that it would place no obstacles in the way of Chinese purchases of military hardware from West European sources.
     There remain issues separating China and the
United States, some of them important. Beijing is
not happy with the fact that Washington has pledged
sales of defensive military weapons to Taiwan (1979
sales totalled about $240 million; sales worth $280
million have been pledged for 1980). Throughout
1979, Vice Premier Deng Xiaoping and other PRC
leaders continued to make overtures to the government and the people on the island, promising extensive economic, political, and even military autonomy in exchange for an abandonment of a separate
status. Unrestricted visitations and communications were suggested, as was economic intercourse.
Taipei refused these overtures but did sanction select conversations with PRC citizens on the part of
its conference delegates and students abroad. The
issue of sovereignty remained a critical obstacle.
     Taiwan is not the only issue separating the
PRC and the US. The two nations are supporting
different sides in Korea. China, moreover, continues to criticize the United States on many issues, especially before Third World audiences. For
example, in Mexico City, the Chinese ambassador accused both the US and the USSR of "endangering
world peace" through their respective actions in
Iran and Afghanistan, and went on to charge that
they were accelerating the arms race and fanning
serious conflicts in the world. The PRC does not
want to be identified too closely with the United
States politically, especially in the Third World.
     Still, Chinese policy toward the superpowers

is clear: the Soviet Union ("social imperialism") constitutes the primary threat of this period, and only the broadest united front, a front including the United States, can counter that threat. Thus, PRC officials applaud a strong NATO and all other evidence of increasing American military power. They hail the positions of such individuals as Senator Henry Jackson and National Security Advisor Zbigniew Brzezinski. Beijing's leaders are not interested in a formal alliance, but they want the United States to serve as a countervailing force to the USSR, and in this global role, to provide protection, at least indirectly, to a China that is destined to be militarily weaker than the Soviet Union for the remainder of this century and beyond.

Like some other nations, the PRC evidences frequent concern over the credibility and durability of the United States as a major power. If the US falters, the PRC will have little choice in the long run to reach an accommodation with nearby Soviet power. For the present, however, that is not the trend.

WEST EUROPE

Chinese policies with respect to West Europe were widely publicized in the course of Hua Guofeng's three-week trip beginning in mid-October 1979. Hua covered the key countries of the region -- France, West Germany, Britain, and Italy -- the first time in history that a Chinese head of state had traveled to the West. Everywhere, the message was the same: "China wants Europe to be strong and united." Out of deference to European leaders, Hua toned down his anti-Soviet remarks in some settings, but there could be no mistaking his primary purpose -- that of emphasizing the Russian threat to West Europe.

Hua also sought to encourage Eurocommunism, thereby fostering a Chinese connection with Communist movements relatively independent of the Soviet Union. It was significant that he chatted informally with Enrico Berlinguer, head of the Italian Communist Party, but made no effort in France to see Georges Marchais, leader of the pro-Soviet French Communists.

Economically, Hua seemed keenly interested in European industrial operations, but it does not appear that major agreements with any of the governments or with private companies were concluded. China has been approaching military and industrial purchases from Europe with caution.

THE ENDURING ISSUES OF CHINESE FOREIGN POLICY

In any survey of Chinese foreign policy, attention must be paid to the three great source
springs of that policy which have endured since the
Communists first came to power: tradition, ideology, and nationalism.

In certain respects, and particularly in their
relations with small neighbors, the Chinese leaders
of today behave very much in the manner of their
ancestors. "Good barbarians" living on their borders are rewarded with praise, their policies supported, and some gifts proffered in the form of
military or economic assistance. "Bad barbarians"
are punished -- and the very word "punishment" used
in connection with the incursion into Vietnam had a
highly traditional ring. Further, modern Chinese
leaders, like those of the past, believe that China
has a natural right to a certain primacy in East
Asia. The "middle kingdom" mentality is by no
means dead, nor is that curious mixture of aloof-
ness (in times of crisis, sometimes taking xenopho-
bic forms) and insistence upon recognition.

When Mao and his associates first came to
power, the ideological quotient in Chinese policy,
both domestic and foreign, appeared to be high.
Spokesmen identified China as firmly in the socialist camp, "led by the Great Soviet Union." There
was much talk -- and some action -- in placing the
PRC on the side of "the global revolution," and the
Chinese established links with various radicals,
including those in guerilla movements, that continue in certain cases to the present. Yet, in recent
years it is clear that the ideological element in
Chinese thought and policy has receded. It still
affects the rhetoric of foreign policy pronouncements, but rarely the substance. Lip service is
still paid to "socialist comrades" and "the global
proletariat," but the central core of Chinese foreign policy is a hard-headed, balance-of-power approach grounded in the leadership's perception of
China's national interest.

In fact, nationalism has triumphed over all
else, as was true earlier in the Soviet Union. A
key objective of Chinese foreign policy is to
achieve greater security in the face of a perceived
threat of major proportions from its massive neigh-
bor to the north and west, the USSR. To this end,
China seeks to offset its weakness by encouraging

the construction of a global united front. More
than a decade ago, Mao and his associates came to
realize that, to be effective, such a front had to
be led militarily by the United States. Identifi-
cation solely with the Third World, as was attempted briefly in the 1960s, served neither the security nor the developmental interests of China.
These two interests, moreover, are closely inter-
twined. If China is ultimately to be the master of
its fate, the processes of nation-building and economic modernization must move forward at an accelerating pace. It is for this reason that Beijing's
leaders have come to the reluctant conclusion that
agricultural and industrial modernization must for
now take priority over military modernization -- a
conclusion likely to be challenged repeatedly by
external events and internal interests, but one
having considerable logic on its side.

Domestic and foreign policies are thus intimately linked, as China begins a massive modernization drive. The fragility of the internal political and economic order demands that risk-taking in
the international arena be limited and carefully
weighed. It argues for the turn toward advanced
industrial nations that has taken place, but with a
greater understanding of the enormous problems involved in transferring modern science and technology into a backward society, and the probable costs
in terms of ideological purity and political unity.
Finally, it cannot be assumed that China's position
in the Sino-US-Soviet triangle is fixed for all
time. The issue of how to live safely with and, if
possible, derive benefits from the world's two gi-
ants will be a recurrent one for China in the decades ahead.

8
Uncertain Future:
Politics in Taiwan

Hung-mao Tien

INTRODUCTION: THE KAOHSIUNG INCIDENT

Kaohsiung, Taiwan's principal industrial port, is a symbol of that island's ambiguous future. The city's prosperity is representative of Taiwan's economic success. But when a demonstration there on December 10, 1979 erupted into violence, it reflected serious political tensions and signalled a potential for instability.

Kaohsiung (pronounced gow-shyung) is the site of an export processing zone, which lures foreign investment through preferential taxation. Its factories -- an amalgam of overseas capital, skilled Chinese management, and a disciplined work force -- produce an increasing volume of goods destined for international markets. Due largely to Kaohsiung (located on the southwest coast) and other industrial centers around the island, Taiwan's foreign trade increased by 33 percent in 1978 and 30 percent in 1979. In 1979, the value of two-way foreign trade ($30.9 billion) was equivalent to 96.6 percent of GNP, and was $1.3 billion in the black. For the first quarter of 1980, two-way trade amounted to $8.9 billion, 31 percent over the same period the year before.

This "economic miracle" has provided Taiwan with a hedge against instability at home and isolation abroad. Its population of 17.5 million enjoys one of the best living standards in Asia (per capita income = $1,720), and income distribution is relatively equal. Foreign investment in Taiwan, now running $2.25 billion (30 percent from the US and 17 percent from Japan), means that political constituencies in other countries have vested interests in the status quo. The economy generates enough of a surplus to finance a well-equipped and well-trained military, including purchases of advanced military equipment from abroad. Kaohsiung is part of Taiwan's way of surviving in a world where it has diplomatic relations with only a handful of nations.

But the December 1979 Kaohsiung Incident raises questions about the island's long-term stability. It was the latest episode in a festering and sometimes violent dispute between the island's Taiwanese majority and the Nationalist Party (Kuomintang or KMT), dominated by mainlanders who retreated to Taiwan after their 1949 defeat at the hands of the Communists. (Taiwanese, who came from the Chinese mainland before the 20th century, constitute 85 percent of the population, and mainlanders the remaining 15 percent.) Politically active Taiwanese -- often called "the Opposition" -- are united in their desire to gain more political power at the Nationalists' expense, but they have disagreed on how to get it. The Nationalist regime (which calls itself the Republic of China) wants to preserve its dominant position, but is divided on how to do so. The Kaohsiung Incident and its aftermath were the climax of the latest phase of this struggle, the first clash since the United States derecognized Taiwan on January 1, 1979.

The Incident grew out of a rally sponsored by activists associated with the magazine Formosa (Mei-li tao in Chinese), who were pressing for rapid political change through confrontational tactics -- rallies, demonstrations, and so on. According to various estimates, anywhere from 5,000 to 30,000 supporters and onlookers gathered for the rally on December 10, 1979, watched by several hundred police, military police, and anti-riot forces. Both sides reportedly tried to observe restraint, but demonstrators and police clashed in a few moments of confusion. Apparently, there were injuries on both sides, but the numbers are a matter of debate.

Why the incident occurred is still unclear. Did some of the organizers precipitate the disturbance? Did the authorities overreact? It does appear that the authorities anticipated trouble, as evidenced by the substantial security forces deployed. Furthermore, poor communication, misperceptions, and unskilled management of the event were at least partially responsible for the outbreak of violence.

Whatever the case, the regime moved quickly to
arrest a number of Opposition leaders -- fourteen
on December 13, three days after the Incident, and
approximately 140 others in subsequent weeks. Formosa and other Opposition journals were closed.
Though the authorities insisted that only those
directly involved in the Incident were targets of
arrest, informed sources indicate that most activists directly connected with the Formosa democratic
movement were arrested, whether they took part in
the disturbance or not. By March 1980, about two-
thirds of those arrested had been released. The
remaining cases have gotten continuous public attention in Taiwan, and have been followed closely
by foreign observers, including Amnesty International. Eight leaders of the Formosa movement were
tried by court-martial during March 1980, thirty-
three others were tried in civilian court in early
April on charges stemming from the Incident, and
ten more went to trial in May, charged with har-
boring one of the leaders.

The origin and consequences of the Kaohsiung
Incident are an integral part of Taiwan's political
evolution, a subject of great importance not only
to the island's residents, but also the governments
in Washington and Beijing. There are three engines
of political change in Taiwan today. First is the
conflict between the Kuomintang and the Opposition.
Second is the division within the Nationalist leadership on how to respond to Taiwanese political
pressure. And third is the effect that the first
two rivalries have on the struggle for succession
to KMT leader Chiang Ching-kuo. What is the substance of these three conflicts? How do they
relate to each other? What are Taiwan's political
prospects?

THE POLITICS OF OPPOSITION

The Nationalists took control of Taiwan in
1945, ending 50 years of Japanese rule. Since that
time, Taiwanese have periodically challenged the
political dominance of the KMT, asserting that
their representation in the regime should more
closely reflect their majority share of the island's population. Some have proposed that the
island should become an independent state. But the
Nationalists have refused to relinquish control of
the critical levers of power, and have used firm
measures at times to preserve their position.
Their rationale, on which they base their claim of

legitimacy, is that the KMT regime is the rightful
government of China, of which Taiwan is a province,
and that it is only temporarily confined to the
island until an opportunity arises to retake the
mainland. Consequently, the regime holds that the
present political structure, established on the
mainland in the late 1940s, should not be changed.
Certain representative bodies (with little political power) should reflect more or less the provincial population distribution of the late 1940s.
This limits Taiwanese entry into these bodies
through elections, as well as appointment to the
much more powerful executive branch.

Blocked in some areas, Taiwanese have progressively increased their influence in others -- with
KMT approval. Taiwanese control the private economic sector, including 90 percent of the island's
foreign trade and all private banks. Even in the
political sphere, their role has grown, often at
the expense of second generation mainlanders. One-
third of the KMT's Central Executive Committee,
three Cabinet ministers, and a number of sub-minis-
ters are Taiwanese. Local government is a Taiwanese domain.

This gradual Taiwanization has not silenced
calls for more fundamental reform. Over the years,
there has been continual opposition to the KMT from
"independents" (tang-wai in Chinese, meaning "outside the Party"), so called because the KMT has not
allowed them to form a political party. Ideologically, the independents run the gamut from liberal
democracy to democratic socialism. They all agree
on the need for greater Taiwanese access to additional political power, and the vast majority
reject "unification" with the mainland. But there
is a range of conflicting views on strategy and
tactics. The more moderate components of the Opposition coalition, led by individuals like K'ang
Ning-hsiang, have advocated working with the KMT to
produce orderly change (an approach quite close to
that of moderate elements within the KMT). Others
have pressed for more rapid change, and have relied
on more public forms of protest to accelerate the
process. The moderate wing has felt that such
pressure tactics will only provoke a counterreac-
tion from the KMT.

In recent years, the various Opposition groups
have drawn their support from the Taiwanese middle
class (which has been increasingly willing to use
its affluence for political ends), from the younger
intelligensia, from socially dislocated workers

whose incomes have not kept pace with general economic growth, from disaffected farmers, and from Taiwanese living in Japan and the United States. That support has been translated into growing Opposition strength in those elections which the KMT permits.

In the most recent elections for local offices, held in November 1977, Opposition candidates captured 4 out of 20 races for county and city executive offices. In the 77-member provincial assembly, their representation increased from 8 seats to 21. Together, independent candidates received 34.6 percent of the total popular vote.

The Opposition's ability to poll such a high percentage was impressive for several reasons:

--it was not allowed to form a coordinated campaign organization, and many candidates were starved for campaign funds.

--the KMT claimed a Party membership of over 1.6 million -- approximately 10 percent of the total population, or close to 20 percent of the eligible voters -- providing firm electoral support.

--the KMT could officially influence the votes of all mass organizations (trade unions, the Youth League, etc.), an extensive bureaucracy, and the armed forces (450,000 personnel and their families).

--KMT candidates enjoyed the advantages of well-oiled campaign machines and the support of the officially controlled mass media.

The 1977 balloting was marred, however, by an incident that occurred in the northwestern town of Chungli. Rumors of KMT ballot-tampering provoked a riot by local residents. A police station was burned down and a number of vehicles were destroyed. It was the first major instance of public violence in twenty years, and helped shape the KMT response to future events.

The Independents next contested elections, scheduled for December 1978, for seats in the nominal parliament. Their candidates often drew large crowds to campaign rallies. Without actually forming a political party, groups in the Opposition mainstream began to create a network of campaign organizations to pool financial and human resources. Most observers agree that the Opposition would have made a strong showing in those elections. But the regime cancelled them after the United States derecognized the Nationalists in mid-December, ten days before the elections were to be

92

held.
Despite the cancellation, the Opposition saw
an opportunity in derecognition. The US action,
which by implication rejected the Nationalists' de
jure claim to represent the mainland, weakened
further the basis of the regime's legitimacy
formula. The Opposition pressed its cause
throughout 1979, with an eye to ultimately creating
a major opposition party. Buoyed by the rising
public concern over the island's future and by social dislocation caused by rapid economic growth,
some elements of the coalition sponsored public
seminars and mass rallies to dramatize the contro-
versy.
In June 1979, the government granted an unex-
pected opportunity -- permission to publish journals that aired independent views. The two major
Opposition periodicals -- The Eighties (Pa-shih
Nien-tai) which appeared in June, and Formosa which
began publication in September -- bridged the
spectrum of diverse views on political, social, and
economic issues. The content was often provocative
and sometimes proposed political action. The Formosa group in particular utilized its magazine's
branch offices to develop island-wide grass-roots
organizations, recruiting activists and organizing
public forums. By early December, Formosa claimed
a monthly circulation of 140,000 copies and had
established eleven regional distribution centers.
It was the Kaohsiung branch that sponsored the
December 10th rally in observance of UN Human
Rights Day.

POLICY DEBATE WITHIN THE KUOMINTANG

There are certain issues on which KMT leaders
apparently agree: the foreign trade orientation of
the economy; maintaining a strong military to
defend against external attack; preserving strong
ties with non-Communist nations even in the absence
of diplomatic relations; and giving a deaf ear to
PRC overtures for a negotiated settlement of
national unification between the mainland and
Taiwan.
But devising a response to the mounting Opposition pressure has seriously divided the Nationalist leadership. Issues of debate include: how
fast Taiwanese should be brought into the upper
levels of the political structure; what institutional changes should be made to facilitate the
process; and whether the regime's legitimacy formu-

la should be revised. Taiwan's ruling circles had already begun to discuss the domestic political implications of US derecognition before it occurred; a public debate ensued in early 1979 and continued throughout the year.

Broadly defined, there have been two principal schools of thought -- loose coalitions of groups and individuals both within the regime (government, Party, and military-security forces) and without (mass media, academicians, and other professionals). One of them can be labeled the tradition- alist-hardliners, who wish to perpetuate the polit- ical status quo. According to well-informed sources, proponents of this school include major military figures (General Wang Sheng), Party ideo- logues (Ku Cheng-kang), some high Party bureaucrats (Chang Pao-shu, Chang Ch'i-yün), advocates of traditional culture (Hu Ch'iu-yuan), and their supporters in the universities and mass media.

The traditionalist-hardliners have echoed Party orthodoxy. They have resisted changes that may lead to the Taiwanization of the regime. They have regarded suggestions that the regime and constitutional order be transformed as politically suspect or even treasonous. And they apparently believe that Taiwanization will lead only to a series of political demands by the Taiwanese major- ity at the expense of the mainlanders.

By contrast, the technocrat-moderates have focused more on the constraints of Taiwan's inter- national environment. They have advocated building Taiwan as a model of economic development and political democracy, and as a contrast to the system on the mainland. This coalition includes senior Party leaders (Huang Shao-ku), technocrats (Premier Y. S. Sun and Party Secretary General Chiang Yen-shih), Western-educated second echelon scholar-bureaucrats (Ch'en Lü-an and Kuan Chung), publishers of some of the major daily newspapers (United Daily News), and an extensive network of academicians (Hu Fo and Shen Chün-shan), business leaders, and professionals.

The technocrat-moderates have advocated var- ious political reforms to strengthen the "Taiwan character" of the regime. Publicly they have not opposed the KMT's orthodox principles. But pri- vately many have deemphasized recovery of the main- land and the Party's "historic mission" for reuni- fication, dismissing any realistic hope for polit- ical reunification with the mainland on the KMT's terms. Thus they have sought a new legitimacy

based on the regime's spectacular economic performance and increasingly democratic government. Calling on the mainland to "learn politics from Taipei," they have advocated building Taiwan as a
model of political liberalization.

In early 1979, some adherents to this technocrat-moderate view began to propose major institutional reforms in newspapers, magazines, seminars,
and conferences. They advocated substantial or
total restructuring of the regime's legislative
institutions to make them more representative of
the island's population. Such "drastic" reform,
the moderates claim, would accommodate growing
Taiwanese demands for political representation and
participation: it would simultaneously facilitate
the broader objective of political democratization.
For the present, however, the hardliners continue to prevail. The Kaohsiung Incident, following the Chungli Incident in 1977, gave credence to
the view that liberalization only breeds instability. Chiang Ching-kuo has apparently ruled in
their favor, at least temporarily. Thus in the
closing session of the fourth plenum of the Party's
11th Central Committee on December 15, 1979 --
after the Kaohsiung Incident -- Chiang did not
discuss changes in the political structure or revision of the legitimacy formula, though he did
announce a marginal increase in Taiwanese representation to legislative bodies. The April 1980
court-martial sentences only confirmed that the
traditionalist-hardliners had scored another
victory.

THE SUCCESSION TO CHIANG CHING-KUO

The challenge of the Taiwanese Opposition, and
the Nationalist debate over how to deal with it,
has inevitably affected the struggle to succeed the
70-year-old Chiang Ching-kuo. Chiang has been the
arbiter of competing views, and there is no sign
that he has cultivated a single successor. Like
his father Chiang Kai-shek, who died on April 5,
1975, he appears to have taken every precaution to
prevent his lieutenants from building their own
power bases. In both the military and civilian
fields, powerful officeholders have been given
short tenure. But Chiang's inevitable passing --
he has diabetes but is thought to be in generally
good health -- could open the way for a successor
with a strong preference on how to deal with the
Opposition.

Information about Chiang's succession has always been limited. But it is clear that General Wang Sheng and Lee Huan were for a time prime contenders. Both are long-time followers and loyal lieutenants of Chiang, but have disagreed sharply on Taiwan's future course.

For a long period, Lee Huan was a principal leader of the technocrat-moderate group. Now 64, he was a graduate of Futan University in Shanghai and studied briefly at Columbia University. In the 1960s, Lee apparently began building a political base by occupying important Party and mass organization positions vacated by Chiang Ching-kuo in climbing to the top. Lee occupied such powerful posts as chairman of the China Youth Corps and of the provincial Party headquarters, head of the Party's central organization department, and director of the Party's upper echelon cadre institute. He was a consistent advocate of broader Taiwanese political participation as a way of preserving the KMT's position, and extended lines of communication to Taiwanese individuals and groups (for example, the Taiwanese Presbyterian Church).

Wang Sheng is a leader of the hardliners. His unusually close association with Chiang Ching-kuo can be traced to the 1939-45 period, when Chiang served as administrative inspector of southern Jiangxi province. Wang, now 63, was a county military chief under Chiang from 1941-45, and subsequently rose through the ranks of the army's political commissariat. Most recently, he was president of the military's political warfare college, a school that trains political cadres for the armed forces. Now director general of the defense ministry's powerful political warfare department, Wang claims the loyalty of an extensive network of politcal officers who manage Party and security matters in the military. He has persistently defended Party orthodoxy, and has seen Taiwanizaion as a serious threat to the regime.

Since 1977, the balance has tipped very much in Wang Sheng's favor. In early 1978, Lee Huan was stripped of all major positions. He was blamed for the Chungli riot (he had been in charge of the November 1977 local elections in his capacity as head of the KMT organization department) and for failing to quiet political dissent voiced by the Taiwanese Presbyterians. Despite Lee's dismissal, the moderates' views on the Taiwanization issue regained much currency during late 1978 and 1979. But the Kaohsiung Incident, besides blocking

further liberalization, gave Wang Sheng another
boost. Thus on December 14, 1979, he was elected
to the Party's central standing committee.

Is Wang Sheng actively setting the stage to
succeed Chiang Ching-kuo? How does Chiang react to
Wang's energetic but quiet empire building? There
are no definitive answers to these questions, but
certain clues are available. Aside from Chiang
himself, Wang is now the only political figure
possessing an institutional power base and a long
list of allies in the military, Party leadership,
KMT bureaucracy, mass media, and leading academic
institutions. The visible accumulation of power by
those parts of the military-security group led by
Wang has left many civilian technocrats and moderate Party bureaucrats increasingly anxious. Some
reportedly have expressed the concern that Wang's
rise might block the process of democratization.
Informed critics have charged that he has deliberately exaggerated to his own advantage threats to
Taiwan's internal and external security.

Chiang's own views on the succession are
difficult to gauge. In his fourth plenum address
in December 1979, he reiterated the regime's stand
to abide by constitutional democracy and he
denounced the possibility of "military rule." His
statement may have been a reference to the October
1979 conspiracy that led to the assassination of
South Korean President Park by ranking security and
military officers. Chiang may also have been
delivering a warning to his ambitious military
lieutenants. It is not inconceivable that he could
once again favor the leaders of the technocrat-
moderates, if they are able to make a strong case
for "guided Taiwanization," and if Wang Sheng over-
plays his hand. But for the moment, a leader of
the traditionalist-hardliner coalition seems to
have the inside track in the succession race.

CONCLUSION: THE KAOHSIUNG INCIDENT REVISITED

During March and April 1980, forty-one of the
Taiwanese activists arrested in the Kaohsiung Incident were brought to trial. Eight demonstration
leaders appeared before a court-martial from March
18 to 28, and were found guilty of sedition.
Thirty-three were tried in civilian court on criminal charges such as disturbing public order and
injuring policemen. In May, ten persons were tried
separately, charged with aiding the escape of one
of the leaders, Shih Ming-te (one of those charged,

Kao Chün-ming, is secretary general of the Taiwan Presbyterian Church).

On April 19, 1980, the court-martial pronounced sentence: Shih Ming-te was sentenced to life imprisonment, and the others received prison terms of twelve to fourteen years.* In early June, sentences for the civilian court cases were announced: one person was acquitted, twenty-two received six-year terms, and the remainder faced terms of ten months or more. Kao Chün-ming and his nine codefendants received two-to-seven year sentences.

The court-martial received widespread attention both in Taiwan and abroad. Although the court proceedings were not open to the public, the authorities allowed reporters, defendants' relatives, and observers (including representatives of international human rights organizations) to attend. Furthermore, Taiwan's newpapers provided unprecedented coverage of the trial, including transcripts of statements and testimony. As a result, Opposition viewpoints probably got more exposure than ever before.

As for court procedure, the court-martial represented a vast improvement over the handling of similar cases in the past. The prosecutor presented some material evidence and the defendants' confessions, obtained by security personnel during pretrial interrogations. Defendants and their attorneys were given some opportunity to present their arguments. All eight defendants repudiated the most damaging parts of their confessions, on the grounds that they were "coerced" through highly irregular interrogation techniques, such as uninterrupted questioning for as long as 80 hours. (All but one did deny rumors that they had been subject to physical torture.) Moreover, the defendants raised fundamental questions about the regime's legitimacy.

During the trial, the prosecutor focused on more than the specific charges. It was clear from the prosecutor's allegations, the five-man tribunal's questions, and the accompanying media campaign that the authorities view the Formosa group's democratic movement as a domestic version of the overseas Taiwan Independence Movement. The regime

---

*Huang Hsin-chieh received the fourteen-year sentence; Yao Chia-wen, Chang Chung-hung, Lin Yi-hsiung, Lin Hung-hsuan, Lu Hsiu-lien, and Chen Chu each got twelve years.

seized on this occasion to make it abundantly clear
that it regards as treasonous the ideas and activities of such movements.

The Kaohsiung Incident and its aftermath have
had a substantial impact on Taiwan's political evolution.   There will continue to be incremental
change, even through the electoral system, but
within newly reinforced limits. On the other hand,
substantial political reform is unlikely any time
soon, given the hardliners' increased power and the
enhanced position of Wang Sheng. The Nationalist
regime will choose security over fundamental political liberalization for the foreseeable future.
Finally, it is not inconceivable that domestic
politics could affect Taiwan's foreign policy as a
consequence of the external environment's effect on
the domestic system.

Even while the trials were in progress, the
Nationalist authorities were preparing a new election law, in anticipation of an election for seats
in the central legislature scheduled for later in
1980. As noted above, Taiwanese representation is
being increased in an attempt to cope with their
discontent. However, campaign activities will be
subject to tighter legal restrictions. Consequently, non-KMT candidates will not be allowed to forge
a coordinated campaign as the Formosa group did.
Democratization via the ballot box will be tolerated only within the regime's constitutional framework. More public forms of political expression,
including demonstrations, will probably not be
tolerated.

The chances of broader political reform --
through a change in the regime's institutions and
legitimacy formula -- are slim for the time being.
The Kaohsiung Incident and the KMT reaction had the
effect of blocking a centrist approach to Taiwan's
future and polarizing the political scene. While
the hardliner group has the upper hand, the
moderate elements within both the KMT and the Opposition will have to suspend their parallel efforts
in support of liberalization, lest their activities
be interpreted as supporting seditious groups.
Those Taiwanese activists who still seek drastic
political change will have to choose between revolutionary action and political withdrawal.

This political situation -- incremental change
within a context of polarization -- is not
necessarily permanent. Much will depend on the
political skill of the moderate elements and the
course set by Chiang Ching-kuo. If this situation

persists, however, a shift in foreign policy is not
out of the question. Recent years have seen growing apprehension about the US as a political and
military partner. Anti-American sentiment is now
pervasive in the media, possibly with official
blessing. Political ideals associated with American democracy are subject to mounting criticism.
As in similar past circumstances, there are rumors
that the Nationalists are quietly exploring other
options, either with Moscow or even Beijing. These
rumors have yet to be confirmed, and may have been
bruited, as in the past, for effect. Whatever the
case, there is no denying the political tightrope
that Taiwan is walking as it enters the 1980s,
faced with an ever-hazardous international environment on the one hand and a delicate domestic
situation on the other.

Appendix A:
Biographical Sketches
of Members of the Politburo
of the Chinese Communist Party

CHAIRMAN

Hua Guofeng

Born in 1920 or 1921 in Shanxi Province, Hua rose to his present position through the ranks of Party and government administrators in Mao Zedong's native Hunan province. In the early 1950s, he served as Party secretary at the county and special district level, and achieved local prominence by virtue of his vigorous sponsorship of the agricultural collectivization movement. By 1958, Hua had become a provincial vice governor and a member of the provincial Party committee, with responsibilities at various times for culture, education, finance and trade, and relations with non-Party groups.

Hua survived the Cultural Revolution to become a vice chairman of the Hunan revolutionary committee in 1968, and then the first Party secretary in 1970. In 1971, he began to appear regularly in Beijing, having been appointed to the staff office of Zhou Enlai's State Council and to a special body appointed to investigate the Lin Biao affair. Hua was elected to the Politburo in 1973 and became a vice premier and minister of public security in 1975. As vice premier, he had responsibility for agriculture and for science and technology, as well as for public security work.

After the death of Zhou Enlai in January 1976, Hua was named acting premier, leapfrogging the two most prominent contenders, Deng Xiaoping and Zhang Chunqiao. After Deng's purge in April 1976, Hua became premier and first vice chairman of the Party Central Committee, reportedly on Mao's proposal.

102

Following Mao's death in September, the "gang of four" sought to block Hua's accession to the Party chairmanship; he responded by placing them under arrest on October 6. Hua's selection as chairman was endorsed by the Politburo on October 7, by the Central Committee in July 1977, and by the 11th Party Congress in August 1977. He also serves as the chairman of the Party's Military Affairs Committee. Hua was confirmed as premier of the State Council by the 5th National People's Congress (early 1978), at which he delivered the report on the work of the government. He is the first person in PRC history to simultaneously hold the positions of Party chairman and premier. Hua visited North Korea in May 1978, and Romania, Yugoslavia, and Iran in August. In the fall of 1979, he traveled to four European countries, being the first Chinese head of state and Party to do so. He attended the funeral of Yugoslav leader Marshal Tito in May 1980, and visited Japan several weeks later.

During February 1980, the fifth plenum of the 11th Central Committee purged four Politburo members (Wang Dongxing, Chen Xilian, Ji Dengkui and Wu De). These four, like Hua, had had close ties to Mao and rose during the Cultural Revolution. Their purge has left Hua as one of the few remaining personalities identified with the Maoist legacy. These recent events suggest that as Deng Xiaoping's allies consolidate their position, Hua's future is likely to become increasingly uncertain.

VICE CHAIRMEN (in rank order; they and Hua Guofeng form the Politburo standing committee)

Ye Jianying

Born in 1898, Ye was a major Communist military figure during the revolution, serving as chief-of-staff of the People's Liberation Army (PLA) in the late 1940s. After 1949, he served as mayor of Guangzhou and governor of his native Guangdong province. With the reorganization of the PLA after the Korean War, Ye was named director of the PLA inspectorate and was elected to the Party's Military Affairs Committee. During the mid-1950s, he was an outspoken advocate of military modernization. He was elected to the Politburo in January of 1967, and became a Party vice chairman in 1973. After the purge of Lin Biao in 1971, Ye was placed in charge of military affairs and was formally named minister of defense in 1975. At the 5th National People's Congress in early 1978, Ye presented the report on the revision of the state constitution. He gave up the national defense portfolio at that time, but became chairman of the standing committee of the National People's Congress (equivalent to head of state). In late September 1979, Ye delivered a major address on the occasion of the 30th anniversary of the founding of the People's Republic. In this address, Ye boldly rejected Mao's definition of revisionism and thereby eroded the underpinnings of the Cultural Revolution.

Deng Xiaoping

Born in Sichuan in 1904, Deng joined the Chinese Communist Party in 1924 while on a work-study program in France. After returning to China, he assumed important posts in the political commissariat in the Red Army, eventually becoming the political commissar of the 2nd Field Army under Liu Bocheng (q.v.). After 1949, Deng served for three years in Southwest China, but was transferred to Beijing in 1952 to become vice premier and to serve for a brief period as minister of finance. In 1954, he became secretary general of the Central Committee, where he was responsible for the day-to-day work of the Party. The following year, he was elected to the Politburo, and his title was changed to general secretary, reflecting an increase in his power.

Deng held both those positions until the Cultural Revolution and was considered, along with Mao, Zhou, and Liu Shaoqi, to be one of the four most powerful men in China. During the Cultural Revolution, he was accused of following "Liu Shaoqi's revisionist line," and was dismissed from office.

Deng was rehabilitated in April 1973, resuming his vice premiership, and was returned to the Politburo in late 1973. Almost immediately, however, his criticism of Cultural Revolution programs and his plans for China's economic development aroused the opposition of radical leaders, who succeeded in having him purged for a second time, in April 1976. After considerable discussion within the Politburo following Mao's death, Deng was restored to office at the third plenum of the 10th Central Committee in July 1977, and gradually thereafter achieved a preeminent political position.

In the fall of 1978, he went to Japan to sign the Sino-Japanese Treaty of Peace and Friendship. The following January, he came to the US, where he signed major science and cultural agreements and discussed the world situation with President Carter. In a February 1980 interview, Deng indicated that he hoped to retire by 1985.

Li Xiannian

Born in Hubei province about 1905, Li was a commander in the People's Liberation Army before 1949. After liberation, he became governor of his native province and held several other important positions in the central-south region. Li was named minister of finance in 1954, succeeding Deng Xiaoping. Within a few months, he was promoted to a vice premiership and placed in charge of all financial and trade matters. In September 1956, Li was elected to the Politburo. He was one of the few high-ranking economic planners to remain in office throughout the Cultural Revolution. He is still a vice premier and was elected a vice chairman of the Party at the 11th Party Congress in August 1977. Since 1949, he has traveled widely in Asia and the Communist world. Li caused quite a stir in mid-1979 when he told Chinese officials that perhaps as many as 100 million citizens had an inadequate diet.

Chen Yun

Chen was born in approximately 1900 (some say 1905) in Jiangsu Province. He participated in part of the Long March, and spent time in Russia in the mid-1930s. In the early 1950s, Chen worked closely with Premier Zhou Enlai on economic affairs, being named the first of ten vice premiers in 1954. Two years later, he was elected to the Politburo and its standing committee, becoming one of China's most powerful half-dozen personalities. In the debates surrounding the Great Leap Forward -- initiated by Mao Zedong in the late 1950s -- Chen continually called for measured, steady, and systematic growth, stimulated by material incentives rather than mass mobilization. This opposition to Mao's policies had by 1961 earned him obscurity, an obscurity that ended only after Mao's demise and the purge of the "gang of four" in 1976. At the third plenum of the 11th Central Committee, Chen was catapulted back onto the Politburo and its standing committee. Formally, he ranks number five in the Party hierarchy. As well, Chen was named the first secretary of the Central Commission for Inspecting Party Discipline. In mid-1979, he was also named a vice premier.

Hu Yaobang

Born in 1915 in Mao's home province of Hunan, Hu Yaobang is a rising star in the Chinese ruling elite, an individual with long-standing ties to Deng Xiaoping. For much of the period since the early 1930s, Hu was involved with Youth League work, becoming head of that organization in the early 1950s. From 1949 to 1952, years that Deng Xiaoping worked in Sichuan, Hu was a key official in the province's northern region. Elected a member of the Central Committee in late 1956, Hu generally spent the next decade in Beijing, except for a brief interlude in Shaanxi province in early 1965 as acting first Party secretary. During the height of the Cultural Revolution, Hu was denounced as a follower of Liu Shaoqi and, as a result of his close ties to Deng Xiaoping, he was on neither the 9th or 10th Central Committees (1969 and 1973).

Only in August 1977 did Hu once again gain membership on the Central Committee. He became director of the Party's powerful organization department late in the year, and a member of the standing committee of the National People's Congress in March 1978. At the third plenum of the 11th Central Committee (December 1978), he became a Politburo member, Party secretary general, and third secretary of the Central Commission for Inspecting Discipline. At about this time, he moved from the Party organization department to its propaganda department. At the February 1980 fifth plenum, Hu was elevated to the standing committee of the Politburo and was acknowledged as head of the newly reconstituted Party Secretariat, in the capacity of general secretary (the post held by Deng Xiaoping prior to the Cultural Revolution). He is no longer director of the Party propaganda department. Hu is one of the half-dozen most powerful leaders in China.

Zhao Ziyang

Born in 1919, Zhao is a veteran Party cadre with extensive experience in south China. Between 1951 and 1955, he was secretary general of the

Party's South China Bureau, responsible for Guangdong and Guangxi provinces. Then, he rose gradually in the Guangdong provincial Party apparatus,
finally becoming first Party secretary in 1965.
Purged during the Cultural Revolution as a "revisionist," Zhao was rehabilitated in 1971 and sent
to Inner Mongolia to serve on the provincial Party
committee there. By March 1972, however, he was
back in Guangdong, and was named first secretary
once again in April 1974. In December 1975, he was
transferred to Sichuan, China's most populous province, to become first Party secretary, chairman of
the provincial Revolutionary Committee, and first
political commissar of the Chengdu Military Region.
Since Deng Xiaoping's July 1977 rehabilitation,
Zhao has rapidly gained political prominence. He
made Sichuan a pacesetter in a number of policy
areas. He was elected an alternate member of the
Politburo at the 11th Party Congress (August 1977),
a full member at the fourth plenum (September
1979), and a vice chairman at the fifth plenum
(February 1980). During late 1979 and early 1980,
Zhao relinquished his government and Party posts in
Sichuan. In April 1980, he became a vice premier,
and it was soon revealed that he had taken charge
of the day-to-day work of the State Council, previously the responsibility of Deng Xiaoping.

FULL MEMBERS (in alphabetical order)

Chen Yonggui

     Born between 1910 and 1920, Chen is the peas-
ant representative on the Politburo. For many
years, he was the leader of the Dazhai production
brigade in Shanxi province -- a unit which was the
national model in agriculture. During the Cultural
Revolution, he became a Party leader at the county
and provincial levels and was elected to the Politburo in 1973. A vice premier, Chen made one of the
major speeches at the national conference on agricultural mechanization in December 1976. In 1978
and 1979, as China's leaders began to emphasize the
modernization and mechanization of agriculture, Dazhai came under a veiled attack and its mobilization techniques fell from favor. In the process of
reevaluating Dazhai, Chen has appeared less frequently in public, suggesting that his role is modest and declining.

Deng Yingchao

Deng is the widow of former Premier Zhou Enlai. She was born in 1903, and is a revolutionary
figure in her own right. Deng participated in the
Long March and has been a constant proponent of
women's rights. During the late 1930s and early
1940s, she (along with Zhou Enlai) was a Communist
representative in protracted negotiations with the
Nationalists. After 1949, Deng was preoccupied
with social welfare policy. She became a member of
the Central Committee in September 1956, but her
position and public appearances were largely honor-
ific in the 1960s. She weathered the Cultural Revolution quite well, being named to all the post-
Cultural Revolution Central Committees. In the
1970s, Deng played an active role in the National
People's Congress as a vice chairman and member of
its standing committee. In December 1978, Deng
rose to Politburo status and was named second secretary of the Central Commission for Inspecting
Discipline. Throughout the post-Mao era, Deng has
traveled widely in Asia, trying to bolster China's
image and offset Soviet gains in the region.

Fang Yi

Born in 1916, Fang's experience in administrative and economic affairs dates back to 1939. Between 1949 and 1953, he served in various posts in
Fujian, Shanghai, and the East China region. He
was transferred to Beijing in September 1953 and
served for a year as vice minister of finance. Between 1956 and 1960, Fang served in Hanoi as the
representative of the ministry of foreign trade.
Upon returning to China, he was named vice chairman
of the state planning commission, deputy director
of the staff office for foreign affairs under the
State Council, and director of the commission for
economic relations with foreign countries. Fang
survived the Cultural Revolution, and was recon-
firmed in the latter position in January 1975. In
January 1977, he was transferred from international
economic affairs to science administration, becoming vice president of the Chinese Academy of Sciences. He was elected to the Politburo at the 11th
Party Congress (August 1977) and became a vice premier at the 5th National People's Congress in early
1978. He is concurrently the minister in charge of
the state scientific and technological commission.
He accompanied Vice Premier Deng Xiaoping on his

January 1979 trip to the United States, and in mid-1979 was named president of the Chinese Academy of Sciences. Fang is said to have heart trouble.

Geng Biao

Born in 1909, Geng was a foreign service officer for most of his post-1949 career, serving as ambassador to Sweden, Denmark, Finland, Pakistan, and Burma, as well as vice minister of foreign affairs between 1960 and 1963. In March 1971, Geng was named director of the Party's international liaison department, responsible for relations with other Communist parties. He was elected to the Politburo for the first time at the 11th Party Congress (August 1977) and in early 1978 he became a vice premier. His dual positions in the State and Party structures make him a major force in shaping Chinese foreign policy, and in May 1980 he traveled to the United States to discuss with American officials the possibility of US-Chinese military cooperation.

Li Desheng

Before the Cultural Revolution, Li was commander of an army unit stationed in Anhui province. A relatively early supporter of some of the more radical Red Guard groups in the province, Li became commander of the provincial military district in December 1967, and chairman of the provincial revolutionary committee in April 1968. Li was transferred to Beijing in 1970 to become director of the general political department of the People's Liberation Army. He was elected a vice chairman of the Party in 1973. In a rotation of military region commanders in 1973, Li replaced Chen Xilian as commander of the Shenyang Military Region. Possibly because of his radical associations, Li lost his Party vice chairmanship in 1975, but he remained on the Politburo, even after the purge of the "gang of four" in 1976. Since that time, Li has come to the public attention through his efforts to solve energy shortages in the northeast, doing so in his capacity as director of the northeast power network. As well, he has played a visible role in trying to eliminate endemic diseases in the region. Clearly though, Li plays a role much diminished in stature from that he played in 1973.

Liu Bocheng

Born in 1892, Liu is one of the Party's veteran military commanders. In the late 1940s, he served as commander of the 2nd Field Army, with Deng Xiaoping as his political commissar. After 1949, Liu became a member of the Party's Military Affairs Committee and director of the training department of the People's Liberation Army until the unit's abolition in 1957. He was elected to the Politburo in 1956, and has served on it continuously to the present day. In his late 80s, Liu is believed to be in very poor health.

Ni Zhifu

The worker representative on the Politburo, Ni is believed to be in his middle to late forties. Raised in Shanghai, Ni moved to Beijing soon after 1949 to work at the Beijing machine tool plant. After spare-time training, he became a worker technician. While active during the Cultural Revolution, Ni was apparently not closely associated with the leftist Cultural Revolution Group. Nonetheless, he was elected to the Central Committee in 1969, to the standing committee of the Beijing Party committee in 1971, and became chairman of the Beijing trade union council in April 1973. He became an alternate member of the Politburo at the 10th Party Congress (1973) and was raised to full membership at the 11th Party Congress in August 1977. After the purge of the "gang of four," Ni was sent to Shanghai, along with Su Zhenhua and Peng Chong (q.v.), to assume the post of second Party secretary. In late 1977, he was identified as the second Party secretary of the Beijing Party committee. Ni is chairman of the national federation of trade unions and has come under sporadic criticism in wall posters for alleged links to the now-discredited Cultural Revolution Left. One indication of Ni's reduced stature is the fact that he was not named a member of the Beijing municipal people's government in late 1979, even though he had previously been on that body's predecessor, the Beijing revolutionary committee.

Nie Rongzhen

Born in 1899, Nie has had an unusual career as a military science administrator. Commander of the North China Field Army in the late 1940s, he served

as mayor of Beijing in the early 1950s, and as acting chief-of-staff of the People's Liberation Army
until 1954. A member of the Military Affairs Committee, Nie became a vice premier in November 1956
and became chairman of the scientific planning commission in May 1957. Although that body was abolished during the Cultural Revolution, it is likely
that Nie has continued to have some responsibility
for scientific matters, possibly through a connection with the national defense commission for science and technology. Nie served on the Politburo
briefly at the beginning of the Cultural Revolution, but was criticized during the Red Guard movement. He became a vice chairman of the National
People's Congress in January 1975, and returned to
the Politburo at the 11th Party Congress (August
1977).

Peng Chong

Peng was born in 1915, and worked as a provincial and municipal official in Fujian and Jiangsu provinces in East China. The mayor of Nanjing
before the Cultural Revolution, Peng became a vice
chairman of the Jiangsu provincial revolutionary
committee in 1968, and a deputy Party secretary in
1970. After the first secretary, Xu Shiyou (q.v.),
was transferred to Guangzhou in 1973, Peng succeeded him. In 1975, Peng became second political
commissar of the Nanjing Military Region. After
the purge of the "gang of four," Peng was sent to
Shanghai to become the third Party secretary. He
was elected to the Politburo at the 11th Party Congress (August 1977). With the death of Su Zhenhua
and the transfer of Ni Zhifu (q.v.) to Beijing,
Peng is now both the first Party secretary of the
Shanghai Party committee and mayor of that city.
In the summer of 1979, he traveled to Western Europe. Throughout 1979, Peng had to deal with students and others demanding the right to return from
rural areas to Shanghai.

Peng Zhen

Born in 1902, Peng was mayor of Beijing when
his May 1966 purge sparked the Cultural Revolution.
As early as 1943, Peng had been head of the Party's
powerful organization department. Peng first became a member of the Politburo in 1945 and was reelected to that body in 1956. At the same time he
was named to the Party Secretariat, ranking imme-

diately behind Deng Xiaoping. On the eve of the
Cultural Revolution, Peng was one of the strongest
political figures in China and some analysts specu-
lated that he might succeed Mao Zedong. But this
prediction proved erroneous, however: Peng was
purged on May 16, 1966 for protecting subordinates
who had made thinly veiled attacks against Mao in
print. In December of that year, he was personally
subjected to humiliating criticism at a mass rally
in Beijing. Only in 1979, as the regime was openly
rejecting the Cultural Revolution and restoring to
power its principal victims, was Peng Zhen rehabilitated. He was named a vice chairman of the standing committee of the National People's Congress at
mid-year and was elevated to the Politburo in September 1979. His main responsibility is the development of the legal system.

Ulanfu

     A Mongol, Ulanfu was born in 1906. From 1949
on, he held all the key positions in Inner Mongolia: governor, commander of the military region,
first political commissar, and first Party secretary. Concurrently, he was vice chairman and then
chairman of the nationalities affairs commission of
the State Council, and also a vice premier. In
September 1956, he was named an alternate member of
the Politburo. Ulanfu was attacked by Red Guards
during the Cultural Revolution and lost all his
posts. Rehabilitated in 1973, he was returned to
the Central Committee at the 10th Party Congress,
and elected a full member of the Politburo at the
11th Congress in August 1977. Shortly before the
congress, it was revealed that he was also director
of the Party's united front work department, responsible for Party relations with minority nationalities and with non-Communist groups, particularly
intellectuals. In June 1979, Ulanfu played an important role in the second session of the 5th National People's Congress, being named the secretary
general for the congress presidium.

Wang Zhen

     Wang Zhen was born in Mao Zedong's home prov-
ince of Hunan in 1909. He has spent much of his
life as an army officer, making his pre-Liberation
mark by having his troops engage in productive labor both to help the civilian populace and meet
their own logistical requirements. Indeed, Wang's

success in making his troops self-supporting and socially useful became known as the "Nanniwan experiment." In 1945, Wang was elected an alternate member of the Central Committee and during the subsequent post-1949 period he was a full member of each Central Committee, both pre- and post-Cultural Revolution. In 1954, Wang was head of the railway corps of the People's Liberation Army and minister of state farms and land reclamation. At the 1975 4th National People's Congress, Wang was named a vice premier, a post he continues to hold. At the December 1978 third plenum of the 11th Central Committee, Wang was elevated to the Politburo. During 1978, Wang traveled abroad, visiting Britain, Switzerland, and Pakistan.

Wei Guoqing

Born around 1914, Wei is a native of Guangxi Province, and is of Zhuang nationality. After 1949, he served briefly in Fuzhou, but returned to his native province as governor in February 1955. In October 1961, he became first Party secretary in Guangxi. Heavily criticized by Red Guards during the Cultural Revolution, he nonetheless survived as governor and first Party secretary. In October 1975, he was promoted to become first secretary of the Guangdong provincial Party committee. He was transferred to Beijing in Septmeber 1977 to serve as director of the People's Liberation Army's general political department. He was elected to the Politburo for the first time at the 10th Party Congress in 1973.

Xu Shiyou

In his mid-70s, Xu is a professional soldier who served as commander of the Nanjing Military Region from 1954 until 1973. Active in Jiangsu province during the Cultural Revolution, Xu became chairman of that province's revolutionary committee in 1968, and first Party secretary in 1971. He was elected to the Politburo in 1969. During the rotation of regional military commanders in late 1973, Xu was transferred out of Jiangsu, losing his provincial positions, and moved to the Guangzhou Military Region. He is reported to have been a strong supporter of Deng Xiaoping and a vocal advocate of Deng's 1977 rehabilitation. Xu played a commanding role in China's February 1979 "punitive" expedition against Vietnam. By early 1980, Xu no longer held his post in Guangzhou. He was in Beijing temporarily, and then in May 1980 appeared in Nanjing amid unconfirmed speculation that he and Deng Xiaoping had had a serious disagreement.

Xu Xiangqian

Born in 1902, Xu is known primarily for his distinguished military career before 1949. In the late 1930s and early 1940s, he was deputy commander of the Eighth Route Army under Liu Bocheng; in the late 1940s, he was an army commander in the North China Field Army under Nie Rongzhen. After 1949, Xu was named chief-of-staff of the People's Liberation Army, but apparently because of ill health never served actively in the position (Nie was acting chief-of-staff in Xu's place). Although a member of the Party Military Affairs Committee, Xu was relatively inactive in the 1950s and the early 1960s. He was director of the Cultural Revolution Group of the PLA for a short period and, like Nie, served on the Politburo briefly during the Cultural Revolution. He was reelected to the Politburo at the 11th Party Congress (August 1977) and became China's minister of defense at the 5th National People's Congress in early 1978. At the same meeting, Xu became a vice premier of the State Council.

Yu Qiuli

Born in 1912, Yu is one of China's principal economic planners. His career combines military service and civilian administration. After 1949, Yu served in the People's Liberation Army in both the northwest and southwest. In the mid-1950s, he was transferred to Beijing to serve as director of the finance department of the PLA. Shortly thereafter, he became political commissar of the PLA's general rear services (logistics) department. In February 1958, he moved out of the army to become minister of petroleum, spending much of the early 1960s opening up the Daqing oil field. In 1965, he was appointed a vice chairman of the state planning commission, and was one of the few ministers to receive Mao's repeated praise. Although he was severely criticized during the Cultural Revolution, Yu survived to become chairman of the state planning commission in October 1972, a position he continues to hold. Yu became a vice premier in January 1975 and was elected to membership on the Politburo at the 11th Party Congress (August 1977).

Since that time, Yu has been a major spokesman for
agricultural mechanization, flexible trade and investment relations with foreigners, and caution in
the rate of capital construction. Yu accompanied
Premier Hua Guofeng on his Fall 1979 four-nation
tour of Western Europe.

Zhang Tingfa

Zhang is a relative newcomer to top-level Party leadership. A professional air force officer,
Zhang was named deputy chief-of-staff of the air
force in 1958 and then promoted to become deputy
commander in 1964. Dismissed during the Cultural
Revolution at the time when Lin Biao's supporters
were favored in the air force, Zhang was rehabilitated as deputy air force commander in July 1975.
He became air force commander in April 1977 and
first secretary of the air force Party committee at
about the same time. He replaced Ma Ning who reportedly had connections to the "gang of four."
Zhang rose to Politburo status in August 1977, never even having been a member of the Central Committee prior to that time.

ALTERNATE MEMBERS

Chen Muhua

Chen's career has been in the commission/min-
istry of economic relations with foreign countries.
A middle-level official before the Cultural Revolution, she became a vice minister in April 1971 and
minister in 1977, after Fang Yi (q.v.) was transferred to the Academy of Sciences. Chen became a
member of the Central Committee at the 10th Party
Congress in 1973, and became an alternate member of
the Politburo at the 11th Congress, replacing another woman, Wu Guixian, a former textile worker
who apparently was too closely tied to the "gang of
four." Chen became the only female vice premier in
the State Council at the 5th National People's Congress in early 1978 and is one of two women on the
Politburo, the other being Deng Yingchao (q.v.).
Chen is head of the State Council's leading small
group on planned birth and she has been the spokes-
person for China's tough new birth control policy.
In mid-1979, it looked as if she might fall victim
to charges of having behaved ostentatiously on a
foreign trip, but by year's end her political trou-

bles looked modest.

Saifudin

A Uighur, Saifudin is one of three minority
members of the Politburo. (The others are Wei Guo-
qing and Ulanfu.) Born in 1915, Saifudin studied
in the Soviet Union, and was actually a member of
the Communist Party of the Soviet Union until he
transferred his membership to the Chinese Party in
1950. Before the Cultural Revolution, he was a
Party and government official in Xinjiang, serving
as vice governor between 1949 and 1955 and as governor from 1955 to the Cultural Revolution. He was
a deputy commander of the military district from
1949 to the Cultural Revolution, and a Party secretary after 1956. A survivor of the Cultural Revolution, he was elected vice chairman of the Xinjiang Revolutionary Committee in 1968, and second
Party secretary in April 1971. Following the purge
of the first secretary in the aftermath of the Lin
Biao affair, Saifudin became first secretary. He
was elected an alternate member of the Politburo in
1973, and retained that position at the 11th Party
Congress (August 1977). He lost his posts in Xinjiang in late 1977 but has retained his alternate
status on the Politburo.

Appendix B:
A Statistical Profile
of Chinese Economic Development

	1957	1977	1978	1979
Revenues and Expenditures (billions of yuan)				
Government Revenues	31.0	91.7	112.1	112[P]
Government Investment	12.6	NA	39.5	39.0[P]
Government Health, Education, Science,and Welfare Expenditures	4.6	9.0	11.3	12.1[P]
Military Expenditures	5.5	14.9	16.8	20.2[P]
Output Data				
Grain (MMT)	196	283	305	332
Fish Products (MMT)	3.12	4.700	4.66	4.305
Cotton (MMT)	1.64	2.049	2.167	2.207
Oil Seed Crops (MMT)	3.8	NA	4.6	5.641
Sugar (MMT)	.864	1.816	2.267	2.5
Bicycles (thousands)	806	7,430	8,540	10,090
Sewing Machines (thousands)	278	4,242	4,865	5,870
Crude Steel (MMT)	5.4	23.74	31.8	34.48
Petroleum (MMT)	1.5	93.64	104.1	106.15
Electric Power (billion KW hrs.)	19.3	223.4	256.6	281.95
Transport				
Freight Turnover (bill. ton kms)	173	757	939	1042
Commerce				
Retail Sales (billion yuan)	47.4	141.0	152.75	175.25

Education Enrollments
(thousands)

University and College	441	620	850	1,020
Technical Secondary Schools	778	680	880	1,199
Secondary Schools	6,281	NA	65,480	59,050
Primary Schools	64,279	NA	146,240	146,630

Health

Hospital Beds (thousands)	364	1,770	1,856	1,932

Source: Chinese State Statistical Bureau and other Chinese
sources.

Notes: Revenue and expenditure data are in current prices.
Grain output, under Chinese definition, is measured in
unprocessed weight, and includes tubers, pulses, and
soybeans. Oil seed crops include only peanuts, rapeseed, and sesame seed.
NA, not available; P, planned level; MMT, millions of
metric tons.

Appendix C:
Romanization Conversion Table

PINYIN TO WADE-GILES/POSTAL ATLAS

Pinyin	Wade-Giles/Postal Atlas
Ai Qing	Ai Ch'ing
Ai Xuan	Ai Hsuan
Ba Jin	Pa Chin
Beijing	Bei-jing/Peking
Bo Yibo	Po Yi-po
Cao Yu	Ts'ao Yü
Chen Muhua	Ch'en Mu-hua
Chen Xilian	Ch'en Hsi-lien
Chen Yonggui	Ch'en Yung-kuei
Chen Yun	Ch'en Yun
Chongqing	Ch'ung-ch'ing/Chungking
Daqing	Ta-ch'ing
Dazhai	Ta-chai
Deng Xiaoping	Teng Hsiao-p'ing
Deng Yingchao	Teng Ying-ch'ao
Ding Ling	Ting Ling
Dunhuang	Tun-huang
Feng Xuefeng	Feng Hsueh-feng
Feng Yuxiang	Feng Yu-hsiang
Fujian	Fukien
Fuzhou	Fu-chou/Foochow
Gan Zegao	Kan Tse-kao
Geng Biao	Keng Piao
Guan Shanyue	Kuan Shan-yueh
Guangdong	Kuang-tung/Kwangtung
Guangxi	Kuang-hsi/Kwangsi
Guangzhou	Kuang-chou/Kwangchow
Hao Ran	Hao Jan
Henan	Honan
Hu Yaobang	Hu Yao-pang
Hua Guofeng	Hua Kuo-feng

Huang Zhen	Huang Chen
Huang Yongyü	Huang Yung-yu
Hubei	Hu-pei/Hupeh
Huxian	Hu-hsien
Ji Dengkui	Chi Teng-k'ui
Jiang Qing	Chiang Ch'ing
Jiangsu	Chiang-su/Kiangsu
Jiangxi	Chiang-hsi/Kiangsi
Li Desheng	Li Te-sheng
Li Keran	Li K'o-jan
Li Kuchan	Li K'u-ch'an
Li Xiannian	Li Hsien-nien
Liang Bin	Liang Pin
Lin Biao	Lin Piao
Liu Binyan	Liu Pin-yen
Liu Bocheng	Liu Po-ch'eng
Liu Shaoqi	Liu Shao-ch'i
Liu Xinwu	Liu Hsin-wu
Lu Xun	Lu Hsun
Mao Zedong	Mao Tse-tung
Meishuyanjiu	Mei-shu Yen-chiu
Nanjing	Nan-ching/Nanking
Ni Zhifu	Ni Chih-fu
Nie Rongzhen	Nieh Jung-chen
Pan Jieje	P'an Chieh-che
Peng Chong	P'eng Ch'ung
Peng Zhen	P'eng Chen
Shaanxi	Shan-hsi/Shensi
Shandong	Shan-tung/Shangtung
Shanxi	Shan-hsi/Shansi
Sichuan	Ssu-ch'uan/Szechwan
Su Zhenhua	Su Chen-hua
Tiananmen	Tien-an-men
Wang Dongxing	Wang Tung-hsing
Wang Zhen	Wang Chen
Wei Guoqing	Wei Kuo-ch'ing
Wei Jingsheng	Wei Ching-sheng
Wenyi Bao	Wen-yi Pao
Wu De	Wu Te
Xinjiang	Hsin-chiang/Sinkiang
Xia Yan	Hsia Yen
Xiao Jun	Hsiao Chün
Xiao Shan	Hsiao Shan
Xu Beihong	Hsu Pei-hung
Xu Shiyou	Hsu Shih-yu
Xu Xiangqian	Hsu Hsiang-ch'ien
Yanan	Yen-an/Yenan
Yangliujing	Yang-liu-ching
Yangzi	Yang-tzu/Yangtze
Ye Jianying	Yeh Chien-ying
Yu Qiuli	Yu Ch'iu-li

Zhang Chunqiao   Chang Ch'un-ch'iao
Zhang Tingfa   Chang T'ing-fa
Zhao Ziyang   Chao Tzu-yang
Zhou Enlai   Chou En-lai
Zhou Libo   Chou Li-po
Zhou Yang   Chou Yang

WADE-GILES TO PINYIN

Wade-Giles   Pinyin

Chang Ch'i-yün   Zhang Chiyun
Chang Chung-hung   Zhang Zhonghong
Chang Pao-shu   Zhang Baoshu
Ch'en Chu   Chen Zhu
Ch'en Lü-an   Chen Lu'an
Chiang Ching-kuo   Jiang Jingguo
Chiang Yenshih   Jiang Yanshi
Chungli   Zhongli
Hu Ch'iu-yuan   Hu Qiuyuan
Huang Hsin-chieh   Huang Xinjie
Huang Shao-ku   Huang Shaogu
Kao Chün-ming   Gao Junming
Kaohsiung   Gaoxiong
Ku Cheng-kang   Gu Zhenggang
Kuan Chung   Guan Zhong
Kuomintang   Guomindang
Lin Hung-hsuan   Lin Hongxuan
Lin Yi-hsiung   Lin Yixiong
Lu Hsiu-lien   Lu Xiulian
Mei-li tao   Meili dao
Pa-shih Nien-tai   Bashi Niandai
Shen Chün-shan   Shen Junshan
Shih Ming-te   Shi Mingde
Yao Chia-wen   Yao Jiawen

Index

124

Housing supply (cont.)
1979 performance, 43-
44
Hu Yaobang, 21, 27-28,
105
Hua Guofeng, 19, 20, 21,
32, 101-02
1979 trip to Europe,
83-84
Huang Yongyu, 56-57, 60
Huang Zhen, 53, 59
"Hundred flowers," 15,
54, 66, 68
Huxian, Shaanxi, 54

Income distribution, 31
wage increases, 40
Independents, Taiwanese
See Taiwanese opposi-
tion to the Kuomin-
tang
Indochina, 76-77
Indonesia, 78
Inequality, social and
political, 5-6, 30-
33, 63
Inflation, 45, 51

Japan
See Sino-Japanese re-
lations
Japanese-Soviet rela-
tions, 79
Ji Dengkui, 27-28
Jiang Qing, 18, 56-57,
59, 71

Kao Chün-ming, 96-97
Kaohsiung Incident,
88-89, 92, 95-96,
96-98
arrests, 89
trials, 96-97
Korea, 78-79
Kuomintang
response to Taiwan-
ese opposition,
92-94, 96-98
succession to Chiang
Ching-kuo, 94-96
technocrat-moderates,

93-94, 98
traditionalist-hardlin-
ers, 93, 94, 98

Labor productivity, 41,
51
Laos, 77
Lee Huan, 95-96
Legal system
PRC, 34, 34-36
Taiwan, 96-97
Li Desheng, 108
Li Keran, 60
Li Xiannian, 104
Lin Biao, 17-18
Literature
attack on socialist sys-
tem, 68-69
broadened subject mat-
ter, 72
critical realism in, 70
liberalization, 65-66
in translation, 65-66
Mao's approach to, 69,
71
political control of,
66, 71-73
resistance to liberali-
zation, 72-73
Underground, 72
"Literature of the wound-
ed," 67
Liu Binyan, 68, 69
Liu Bocheng, 14, 15, 17,
109
Liu Shaoqi, 11, 16, 27
Liu Xinwu, 67, 69
Lu Xun, 65, 69-70

Malaysia, 78
Mao Zedong
approach to art, 54
approach to literature,
69, 71
post-1976 attack on po-
litical legacy, 20-
23, 25, 26-28, 31, 53
relationship with Deng
Xiaoping, 11, 13-14,
15-17, 18